kid
stories

Biographies of
20 Young People
You'd Like to Know

By Jim Delisle

Edited by Pamela Espeland

Free Spirit PUBLISHING

Library of Congress Cataloging-in-Publication Data
Kidstories : biographies of 20 young people you'd like to know /
   [compiled] by James Delisle ; edited by Pamela Espeland.
      p.   cm.
      Includes index.
      Summary: Life stories of twenty school-age boys and girls who were
   brave, intelligent, inspirational, or simply friendly, as they faced things that
   each of us faces.
      ISBN 0-915793-34-2 :
      1. Teenagers—United States—Biography—Juvenile literature.
   2. Children—United States—Biography—Juvenile literature.
   [1. Students. 2. Biography.]   I. Delisle, James R., 1953-
   II. Espeland, Pamela, 1951-   III. Title: Kid stories.
   IV. Title: Kid's stories.
   CT217.P29 1991
   920.073—dc20   91-18363
                                                                            CIP
                                                                             AC

10 9 8 7 6 5 4 3 2
Printed in the United States of America

Cover and book design by MacLean & Tuminelly
Cover photo illustration by Suzanne Brill

Free Spirit Publishing Inc.
400 First Avenue North, Suite 616
Minneapolis, MN 55401
(612) 338-2068

Dedication

To the child you are now, or you were once, this book is dedicated. Each of you is a kidstory-in-the-making. Each of you has a life worth sharing with others.

And to Matt, *my* life's favorite kidstory, this book is for you.

Acknowledgments

The young people who are profiled in this book were all recommended by someone. In some cases (with Jerry Simmons, Natalie Phillips, and Jennifer Engel), I recommended them myself. But generally, it was colleagues and friends who introduced me to the kids and teenagers whose lives fill the pages of this book.

So...thanks to the following people, each of whom knew quality when they saw it in the lives of the young people included in *Kidstories*.

Norma Belasco
Joan Borovicka
Darlene Freeman
Sandra Hinojosa
Charlene Johnson
Abbe Krissman
Martin Laster
Debbie Lerner
Anne McCalpin
Betty Meckstroth

Carol Nighswander
Ralph Pirozzo
Nancy R. Prinzi
Ann Robinson
Mary Starnes
Diana L. Stender
Vicki Stephenson
Gary Swalley
Jan Viars

CONTENTS

THE FINE ART OF ACCEPTANCE   7

1

2

3

TAKING CHARGE OF YOUR OWN EDUCATION

17

GRACE UNDER PRESSURE,
AND UNDER WATER:

LESSONS FROM THE EMERALD CITY   135

18

RUNNING FOR GLORY:

19

STANDING UP FOR ANIMAL RIGHTS:

20

LESSONS LEARNED AT SUMMER SCHOOL:

INTRODUCTION

Biographies—stories of people, tales of lives—are common to us all. Using ourselves as examples, each of us could teach lessons to others. We could give advice about the best ways to avoid trouble (or how to find it). We could calm nerves (or fray them), soothe pain, or teach lessons. Because our lives are each so different and distinct, only we are able to tell the full picture of the individual we were once, we are now, and we hope to become later.

Sadly, most people never get the chance to share their life stories with others. Prove it to yourself: Look in the library, on the shelf labeled "Biographies." There you'll find volumes about George Washington, Eleanor Roosevelt, and Leonardo da Vinci. But do you find any titles like *Cathy Miller, High School Scholar* or *George MacDonald: A Farm Boy Speaks Out*? No. Instead, you find life stories of famous dead people. Seldom, if ever, do you see books written about kids who could be your next-door neighbors, and even more rarely will you locate a book about the actual life of a real teenager (except for royalty, rock stars, and your occasional genius).

Of course, there is a lot we can learn from dead people, famous or otherwise. But there's also a lot we can learn from each other. People don't have to be famous to be role models, nor do they have to be grown up to teach us lessons. Because I believe that kids can learn a lot from other kids, I decided that it was time for a book like *Kidstories*. I hope you agree.

But first, a little personal history (since this is a book of biographies, this only seems natural). I've been a teacher, of kids and adults, for longer than some of you have been alive. Also, I've been a counselor of intelligent kids who didn't "go to school well"—they slid by with okay grades, but their minds and spirits were far removed from the classes they attended. And, not so incidentally, I've been a parent, an uncle, a younger brother, a neighbor, and myriad other roles that involve communicating with kids.

In each of these settings, I have come to respect what I can learn from young people. Even when it was my job to be "the teacher," I still found that almost every child I met offered me a chance to learn something about myself, my life, and my world. I came to realize that the ability to impart knowledge or insight is not limited to persons above the legal age; that given the proper setting, and the willingness to admit our common bonds of humanness, I could just as readily learn from a 12-year-old as he or she could learn from me.

Thus, this book. *Kidstories* gives you the chance to get to know, and learn from, a collection of persons not too unlike yourself in age, intellect, or disposition. As you read these life stories, you will find some of them easier to identify with than others. That's to be expected. Your own life and past experiences will probably cause you to focus on a biography of someone like you—or, perhaps, the type of person you would like to be. My goal for you, as you read the stories that follow, is that you gain an appreciation for a reality that is often ignored by others; that is, that you come to respect, enjoy, appreciate, and learn from the everyday kids who surround you within these pages, within your neighborhood, and throughout our world.

Take care, and may your life be as filled with welcome and unexpected lessons as mine has been.

Jim Delisle
August, 1991

A SPECIAL MESSAGE FOR TEACHERS

What do the following classroom activities have in common?

- Writing about the life of your favorite president

- Holding a "meeting of the minds" debate between various authors and historical figures

- Reading about a famous athlete, actor, or politician, and presenting an original play "starring" this person

- Designing a bulletin board based on the theme, "Great Mistakes of Famous People"

Each of these activities focuses on the lives of individuals who have left a mark on our world—people who, for better or worse, have changed the way we think or act, or who have influenced world events enough that they are remembered by future generations.

Teachers are aware of the powerful impact biographies can have on students' learning. For example, when students read that Helen Keller's accomplishments were achieved despite her physical handicaps, or that Tom Cruise's learning disability made him think he was dumb, they are able to see that success is seldom achieved swiftly or without effort. Biographies help teach students that even successful and famous adults were all once children; children who attended school, played sports, and argued with their parents about curfews and cleaning their rooms.

The reason I compiled *Kidstories* was to show school-age students that they can learn from one another as well as from famous adults. In the life stories that follow, you will read about children who did something as simple as being friendly toward a new classmate from a foreign land; as harrowing as getting emergency help for a child who had just been struck by a car; as exciting as preparing a scientific experiment that will fly on the space shuttle; and as inspirational as raising thousands of dollars to promote breast cancer awareness. Each story is a mini-version of the realities of life each of us faces: the trauma, the joy, and the self-questioning that we all go through when we attempt to make a difference in our lives or the lives of others.

A Few Words About the Format

In compiling this book, I heard from hundreds of young people who had stories to share. Selecting the 20 biographies included here was a difficult task, but my "bottom line" criterion was diversity—diversity of age, location, and story content.

Divided into five categories, the biographies are classified by theme. I'm sure that some of you might think my classification system is arbitrary, as one life story might appear to fit into more than one category. Of course, this is true; no life is ever so "neat and clean" that it fits perfectly into any one category. However, it is my hope that this initial classification system will guide you toward particular biographies that focus more on social acceptance, school-based issues, or overcoming obstacles. Still, each story contains multiple meanings and can teach a variety of lessons, so feel free to set up your own categories as you read them.

Each biography is subdivided into four sections: "Family and Background," "Making A Difference," "Lessons Learned," and "Personal Goals, Global Concerns." This was done to make it easier for you to compare similar themes across the biographies. Rather than put the subheadings within the body of each story (which, I thought, would interrupt the narrative), I have placed them in the margins. Let me know what you think of this technique.

The "Questions to Consider" following each biography are meant to serve as discussion starters among groups of students, or as reflective afterthoughts for individual readers. Certainly, more questions than those included here could be asked about each biography; my questions are merely ideas to "prime the pump" for thinking about or discussing the stories. Further, the "Resources" section gives readers a few places to look if they want more information about particular aspects of each biography.

Regarding the resources suggested: regrettably, some of the best books mentioned are out of print. Many may still be available in school and public libraries. If you *really* want a particular resource and you can't find it anywhere, contact the publisher named in parentheses after the title. Perhaps the book has been reissued in a new edition under a new title. To find additional resources, I strongly recommend *The Bookfinder: A Guide to Children's Literature About the Needs and Problems of Youth Aged 2–15* by Sharon S. Dreyer. Published by American Guidance Service since 1977, this wonderful reference for teachers (currently in four volumes) describes and categorizes current children's books. Look there to find more books on specific themes or topics.

The final section of *Kidstories* includes the "Biographical Sketchbook" I used to gather stories from my respondents. It was a very effective questionnaire, yielding valuable and complete information. Feel free to use this form with your own students, and please consider sending copies of their biographies to me. Perhaps they'll appear in the next edition of *Kidstories*!

I have learned a lot about myself and my profession in completing this book. But perhaps the most valuable lesson of all was being reminded once again of the power, energy, and sensitivity that is alive in the students we teach. May you, too, be inspired by the biographies that follow.

Jim Delisle
401 White Hall
Kent State University
Kent, OH 44242

THE FINE ART OF ACCEPTANCE

Everyone wants to be liked, and everyone wants to be popular. I haven't yet met a person who, upon waking up each morning, yawns, stretches, and thinks, "I wonder how many people I can manage to get to hate me today."

Acceptance. It's as basic as the need to eat, sleep, or smile.

You're about to meet some young people who struggled with acceptance—their own, or someone else's. One thing you'll learn, I think, is that sometimes the price of being popular is so high that you have to decide whether it's worth it.

Something else you might learn from these three biographies is that the best way to make a friend is to be a friend. Maybe that sounds like something a parent or counselor might tell you, or a quote you might read on a $1.59 poster from a Hallmark store. But remember, *everyone* wants to be liked and respected by others. That includes the kid wearing the pocket protector, and the tough-edged bully whose idea of a good time is scraping the chalkboard with her fingernails in sync with the music on her Walkman. In their own ways, in their own styles, even these kids want to be popular.

Beneath our layers of plastic, or leather, or denim, we all would rather be liked than disliked by others.

One more thing you might learn from these stories: It's not always easy to be happy and popular at the same time.

I

LIFE GOES ON AFTER THE PROM:
The Story of Melissa Joy Hinojosa

Melissa Joy lives in Laredo, Texas, a city of about 100,000 people on the U.S. side of the Rio Grande River. Because of its location, Laredo is called "The Gateway to Mexico." As you would expect, the character of Laredo is influenced a great deal by the Spanish culture.

A high school senior in a building that houses 2,800 students, Melissa lives with her parents and her two brothers, Robbie and David. Recently, Melissa was named Texas Young Woman of the Year, and will soon compete as her state's representative in the America's Young Woman of the Year pageant (the former Junior Miss program).

Along with the Texas Young Woman award came $153,000 in college scholarship offers, leaving Melissa many college options from which to choose. In honor of her accomplishments, Melissa was asked to ride as a special guest in the Governor's Inaugural Parade in Austin. Meanwhile, Melissa was named one of Laredo's outstanding citizens, and across the state border in New Mexico, she was chosen Outstanding Attorney at the Youth Legislative Session.

In high school, Melissa has been head cheerleader, a senior class officer, and an officer in the National Honor Society. Her hobbies include horseback riding, fishing, hunting for arrowheads, and performing Cherokee Indian sign language.

MAKING A DIFFERENCE

With Melissa's long list of achievements, you might think her biggest problem would be selecting the one that is most memorable and important to her. When you're good at so many things, and recognized by so many people, it can be hard to choose the single accomplishment that instills the most personal pride.

For Melissa, though, the choice was easy. Her greatest source of pride came as a result of her *not* being selected as a member of the eighth-grade Prom Court.

Huh?

This one can only be explained by learning about Melissa's dilemma. Here is the way she tells it.

"In middle school, I was the host-reporter for a children's news program aired weekly on our local ABC-TV station. I was a cheerleader, President of the Student Council, winner of a Presidential Academic Fitness Award, and I had been voted 'most popular' by my class. I had all these things, yet I had one more goal: to be a member of the eighth-grade Prom Court. Eighth-grade prom was a *very big deal* in my school.

"To be nominated for the Prom Court, you had to be chosen by your home room, and ours was 'ruled' by one big, overaged bully. He approached me in class and said, 'If you want the nomination, take this.' He then showed me a small packet of white powder that was inside his sock. 'Take it,' he said, 'or are you chicken?'

"I had a little time to think about this, because the home room election wasn't until the next day. I didn't think there was anything in the packet except sugar or salt, because drugs were expensive—especially a whole packet full!

"My dilemma was this: If I took the packet and got rid of it right away, no one would ever know, and I'd get nominated. Even if someone told on me, I could probably get away with it because no one would suspect an honor student like me of having drugs. Still, I knew that was wrong."

Melissa didn't take the packet, and when she arrived home that afternoon, she told her parents the whole story. Since they were on a business trip in Colorado, she had to tell them her dilemma over the telephone. Naturally, they were upset. And although they understood their daughter's dilemma, they told her something that, deep down, Melissa already knew: There was no way she could take the packet, even if she did suspect that its contents were harmless.

"The next day arrived," Melissa recalls. "The moment came for the election. I just looked at the class bully. I put my head on my desk. I couldn't take the packet. I didn't get nominated."

At the time, Melissa was confused and saddened by this series of events. She had always been popular and successful in school, and to have her final middle school experience be so negative was something she found very difficult to accept.

Choosing to attend her prom only long enough to get her picture taken, Melissa and her date ended up at the local Baskin-Robbins for ice cream. They were joined by another couple who

LESSONS LEARNED

had learned of Melissa's dilemma and decided that they, too, would boycott the prom. "They had the guts to care," Melissa said, "and I really appreciated that."

Meanwhile, back from Colorado, Melissa's parents approached the school administrators to voice their concern about this incident. However, since Melissa never actually took the packet, the administrators said her story was "hearsay," so nothing was done to address the problem.

Melissa's sadness eventually turned to anger, and when she entered high school that fall, she decided that she would be a different type of student than she had been in middle school.

"I just faded into being a plain student," she says. "I didn't join any organizations at first. What for? It hadn't helped me in middle school. I wasn't going to give people another chance to use me....This was my way of rejecting others."

Her grades were still excellent, but for almost two years Melissa kept her distance from any school activity that would showcase her talents. Then she and her brother, David, heard about a special event to be staged in San Antonio, a city 153 miles from Laredo.

"Peace Child" was a musical-fantasy stage production, a play about friendship, global cooperation, and establishing peace between countries. Starring elementary and secondary school students from the Soviet Union, "Peace Child" was touring America. For the San Antonio performance, a choir of U.S. singers was needed. Despite the more than 300-mile round trip, David and Melissa decided to participate in this choir.

The overall performance was a rousing success, and it helped put Melissa back on the path toward active participation in school and community events. As she explains, "It was a great experience. I began to see that sometimes you have to take a stand for things: peace, the environment, against drugs. It has taken me years to realize that, sometimes, taking a stand hurts. However, life goes on. And if you really believe in and try to reach your goals, you will reach them."

kidstories

Her experiences with "Peace Child," and her eventual success both in high school and in outside activities, have led Melissa to wish for a world in which people were closer, kinder, and more understanding of individual differences.

"I'd like for schools to be smaller," she says, "so that people (students and teachers) could understand each other and could really show each other that they care. Also, I would stop world pollution, as we are killing ourselves and our world at the same time."

When Melissa reflects on her dilemma in middle school, and the decision she might have made, she realizes how right she was in refusing to accept the white powder she was offered. "Now that I have been awarded over $153,000 in college scholarships," she says, "people call me a role model. I tremble when I think that everything might have been different if I had chosen 'the packet.'

"I look forward to the future, knowing that one student *can* stand up for what he or she believes. One student *can* make a difference not only in his or her own life, but in the lives of those who are watching.

"Life goes on after the prom...."

Questions to Consider

1. Some people might think, "Melissa had so much going for her, why should she even care about the Prom Court?" How would you respond to someone who said this about Melissa's dilemma?

2. If you were Melissa's home room teacher, and you found out about the problem Melissa had with the class bully, what would you have done? How would you have reacted—to Melissa, the bully, the rest of the class?

Resources

Melissa and her brother, David, enjoyed singing in the "Peace Child" play. This play is a project of the National Peace Child Foundation. To find out more, write or call:

The National Peace Child Foundation
3977 Chain Bridge Road
Fairfax, VA 22030
(703) 385-4494

Melissa was strong enough to "just say no" to the mysterious packet. It helped that she was popular and successful in school, so her self-esteem was high. She also had her parents' confidence and trust.

The "Just Say No" Foundation gives young people information and support to resist peer pressure and other influences to use drugs. To find out more, write or call:

The "Just Say No" Foundation
1777 N. California Boulevard
Suite 210
Walnut Creek, CA 94596
(415) 939-6666

The library is a great place to educate yourself about drugs. You'll find nonfiction books that give you the facts about all kinds of drugs. And you'll find dramatic fiction books—novels—about kids who learned firsthand what drugs can do. Check your library for these books, and ask your librarian for other recommendations:

The Drug Alert Series (Twenty-First Century Books, 1990-1991). These books may seem too young for you, but they're full of important facts. Look for books on alcohol, marijuana, cocaine and "crack," nicotine and caffeine, steroids, medicines, and more.

Kathleen, Please Come Home by Scott O'Dell (Houghton Mifflin, 1978). Kathleen alienates her family and herself when she is influenced by her new friend to try drugs.

That Was Then, This Is Now by S.E. Hinton (Viking Press, 1971). Mark is like a brother to his friend, Bryon. When Bryon discovers that Mark is pushing drugs, he decides to turn his friend in to the police.

Nikki 108 by Rose Blue (Franklin Watts, 1972). Nikki is a gifted junior high student in the ghetto who is affected by her brother's death from a heroin overdose.

2

REACHING OUT TO A STRANGER:
The Story of Paul Raccuglia

Paul's family sounds like it belongs in a 1950's TV situation comedy. Besides Paul, who is nine, there are his parents and a brother and sister (Paul is the middle child). Pets abound: Jasper and Casper, the cats; a dog named Madison; a bunny, Mary Jane; and a fish called Vicki.

FAMILY AND BACKGROUND

A fourth grader at Red Bridge Elementary School in Kansas City, Missouri, Paul enjoys most sports, but especially soccer. Both in and out of school, he likes math, writing, and using the computer. Other activities that keep him busy include collecting baseball cards, reading *Hardy Boys* adventures, and participating in Cub Scouts.

Paul has plans to become a professional baseball player because, he says, "it's a fun sport and I might like to travel a lot." He has already been doing some traveling, as his family has moved four times since Paul was born. "Three times," Paul observes, "we have lived in green houses."

MAKING A DIFFERENCE

Maybe it's because Paul has moved so many times, or maybe it's the influence of his family's attitudes and values, but the one thing Paul is best at—and most proud of—is his ability to be a good friend to other kids. Especially those most in need of a friend.

"I helped a new boy in my class whose name is Shahab," Paul explains. "He came here from Afghanistan, and he did speak English in a different kind of way. I helped him with his papers and some of the things he didn't know. I played with him at recess a lot. We got to be friends."

In this one short statement, Paul shows how even the smallest display of kindness—talking with "the new kid," playing with him, assisting him with schoolwork—can be an important step in helping another person feel accepted. For Shahab, facing new kids, a new school, a new language, and a new culture all at once must have been a very scary situation. A good friend like Paul was probably just what he needed to feel really welcome in the United States.

What puzzles Paul is why everyone, throughout the world, doesn't share his attitude of being nice to strangers. He would like to see people everywhere treat other people kindly and keep their promises. "I would just say that if you want to help someone you should be nice to them, and you should stick to what you say you will do," he says.

Of course, there were times when it was not always easy to play the dual roles of friend and helper. As Paul discovered, Shahab would sometimes go and play instead of "paying attention when I was helping him with his work." It was then that Paul would call in the reinforcements, especially his teacher, Mrs. Lerner. She had originally asked Paul to help Shahab with his work, and she had assigned the boys seats next to each other. Together, Mrs. Lerner and Paul were usually able to get Shahab back to his work.

P aul may have helped teach Shahab some important school lessons, but Paul also learned a few lessons of his own. There is one in particular that many world leaders have yet to recognize.

LESSONS LEARNED

"I learned sometimes that it can be fun to help somebody," Paul says. "It felt good because I helped Shahab and he became a good friend to me. I learned that people from different countries can be a lot like you."

It's such a simple thing: befriending someone who needs a friend. Yet it's often the simple lessons like this that teach us about life's most important facets.

It seems that Paul and Shahab will continue to be good friends. Paul respects that his new friend "shares stuff, plays with people, and doesn't hit people usually. But when he does get into a fight, later on he will apologize."

W hen Paul considers his own future (in addition to becoming a baseball player), he has several wishes for himself and the world around him. Specifically, he would like to own a baseball card shop, and he wants to continue learning about computers "because it's fun to write stuff."

PERSONAL GOALS, GLOBAL CONCERNS

Paul thinks his school, as good as it is, could be improved by "adding some new playground equipment" and by extending the time he could spend "in special classes—gym, music, library and art." And his home (actually, his backyard) would be better "if someone would fill up the creek and change the steep hills."

Paul's global concerns show that he thinks very deeply about the world. "I wish there wasn't so much pollution," he says. "I wish people would not kill animals just for fun. I wish people would recycle their trash. I wish that white people would treat the black people equal. I wish everyone would have shelter and food to eat."

Underlying every one of Paul's concerns, and each of his wishes, is an attitude of respect: respect for Shahab, respect for the world's less privileged people, respect for life in all its varied forms. With these beliefs serving as his foundations, Paul will continue to make his world and ours a more secure, trusting, and humane place to live.

Questions to Consider

1. Everyone, at one time or another, has been "the new kid." Maybe your family moved, or you were the newest member of a club or a team, or you went to a party where you didn't know anyone except the person who invited you. When you were "the new kid," was there someone like Paul to help ease your adjustment? What did this person do to make you feel more comfortable? Or have you ever played the role Paul did for Shahab? What did you do for "the new kid," and how did it make you feel?

2. Are there any students in your school who may have a hard time fitting in because they appear to be different? Who are some of these students, and what special activities or programs exist to make it easier for them to feel accepted in your school? (Idea: If no such special arrangements are made for new, incoming students, talk with your teachers, principal, and former "new kids" about what can be set up.)

Resources

Some kids might not want to be friends with a boy from Afghanistan who speaks English in "a different kind of way." But Paul reached out, and he made a difference in the world. Now Paul knows that kids from Afghanistan are human, too. And Shahab knows that American kids can be friendly and kind.

You can make a difference in the world, and you can get adults to help you. Have your parents or teachers write or call:

**Parents, Teachers, and Students
for Social Responsibility
P.O. Box 517
Moretown, VT 05660
(802) 223-3409**

If you enjoy making friends with people from other countries and cultures, you should know about AFS. Have you ever heard of "exchange students"? Then you already know something about this organization. AFS places high school students with "host families" in other countries. Maybe an AFS student could live with your family. Or maybe you could be an AFS student yourself one day. To find out more about AFS, write or call:

**AFS International/Intercultural Programs
313 E. 43rd Street
New York, NY 10017
(212) 949-4242**

Legacy International works to promote global understanding and environmental action. This organization also offers an International Summer Leadership Training Program. To find out more, write or call:

**Legacy International
346 Commerce Street
Alexandria, VA 22314
(703) 549-3630**

The Concordia Language Villages are summer camps that promote peace through understanding of other countries and cultures. Language, food, games, music, celebrations, and more give campers the experience of visiting a foreign country. The villages are all in Minnesota, but campers feel as if they're in China, Denmark, France, Germany, Japan, Spain, Norway, even Russia! The Language Villages also sponsor programs abroad. For more information, write or call:

**Concordia Language Villages
901 South Eighth Street
Moorhead, MN 56562
(800) 247-1044 (inside Minnesota)
(800) 222-4750 (outside Minnesota)**

3

THE IMPORTANCE OF FRIENDS:
The Story of Ryan Walter

T hirteen-year-old Ryan Walter lives in Greenfield, Wisconsin, a suburb of Milwaukee. He's in his last year—eighth grade—of Greenfield Middle School, a school Ryan reports as having "interesting special arts classes, a great band and physical education program, and fine hot lunches." (Now, *that's* unusual!)

FAMILY AND BACKGROUND

Ryan lives with his mom and his younger sister, and even though his parents got divorced when he was three years old, Ryan still visits his dad almost every weekend.

Ryan enjoys his neighborhood because, he says, "it is quiet, close to a nature area, and all the important places are within walking distance: malls, supermarkets, restaurants, and movie theaters. That's food, entertainment, and a place to hang out. What else is there in life?" And even though Ryan's home is located in a low-income housing area, he loves it because "my family and I waited five years for a vacancy. This is the nicest place I've ever lived."

Growing up in a lower-class, one-income family, Ryan cannot afford a lot of expensive clothes or shoes, "so I make do with what I have." Still, he wishes people weren't so materialistic or ready to judge someone else by what they are able to afford. "I am an outcast in the eyes of some people," Ryan explains, "and I deal with those individuals by keeping my distance from them. I wish people could look past the labels and take a peek at the person."

MAKING A DIFFERENCE

By separating himself from others who seemed to judge him before they even knew him, Ryan was alone more often than he liked. He began to substitute companionship with real friends by reading—in fact, by reading a lot.

"I had always liked reading," he explains, "but I never thought books could act as the companionship and enjoyment I lacked in my life. I sometimes read 500 pages a day. Even though those years were the loneliest, most depressing years of my life, I was gaining a lot of knowledge."

That was when Ryan was younger. Today he feels both well-liked and respected. In fact, he considers his new-found social acceptance to be one of his life's greatest accomplishments.

How did this happen? How was Ryan transformed from a social isolate into someone with friends and classmates who respect him? Ryan gives that credit to many people, but especially to Mrs. Jane Carter, his fifth-grade teacher.

Mrs. Carter recognized Ryan's talents in writing, and she put him in charge of the Thanksgiving class play. This, according to Ryan, was the beginning of the end of his social isolation.

"When I wrote, directed, narrated, and cast the play, that's when my peers started taking me seriously," he remembers. "I was no longer a brainy stiff in the eyes of my classmates. Now I was the man in charge, the boss. What the audience saw on the day of the play could have been whatever I wanted it to be. And when everyone had fun and enjoyed the play, people realized that I could be interesting and fun. I gained a lot of friends during that experience."

Ryan also participated as a team member for his school's Future Problem Solving Program. (Kids in FPSP try to solve environmental, political, economic, and other problems that might exist in future years.) He began to see how his talents could help his team members reach their common goals.

His FPSP "coach," Mrs. Abbe Krissman, gave him pointers on how to be a useful team member. "She made me feel special," Ryan recalls, "and many times she seemed to have more confidence in me than I had in myself." Other school people strengthened Ryan's self-esteem. Mr. Harris, Ryan's fourth-grade teacher who had traveled the world, shared his experiences with Ryan and showed him a life very different from the one Ryan knew in Greenfield. And Mrs. Starnes, Ryan's guidance counselor, became his confidant. "She's one of the only people I've really opened up to while talking about myself," Ryan says.

Through the help of many adults in his school, Ryan was able to survive what he calls his "blunder years." After the play and his FPSP project, Ryan says he found the missing pieces of his jigsaw puzzle: popularity and respect. "My life was on the fast track now, and I realized that I no longer needed books as replacements for friends. I had the real thing."

Now a teenager, Ryan looks back on what he did right—and wrong—during his "blunder years." He realizes that the secrets to success and popularity aren't really secrets at all.

"When I was younger, no matter what I tried, I couldn't be accepted by my peers," he explains. "I acted like them, talked like them, and took part in the same activities other people did, but with all that effort I still lacked one thing: acceptance." It was only when he joined some team activities, provided leadership through the school play, and started talking with adults he trusted and respected that Ryan found what he had been looking for. He learned how to enjoy his life more than he ever thought he could. In fact, he now enjoys basketball and baseball—team sports—as well as swimming and video games.

His advice to other kids who are having social troubles? "Don't ever let books become the foundation of your life. There are more important things in life than reading—like friendship and having fun. Of course, you learn from books, but the knowledge you gain by looking and listening to the world around you is far more important."

Having fulfilled some of his personal goals, Ryan hopes there will be some changes in the world around him—the world Mr. Harris has seen so frequently. "If I could change one thing in the world," Ryan says, "it would be to stop all conflict, whether it be between two countries or worse, within a family. How can we live in a peaceful world when some families can't even get along? The solution to world peace doesn't lie in treaties or nuclear weapons; it lies in the ability to deal with and respect one another."

Ryan has learned that self-respect is as important as respect for others. And thanks to the help of people at school, he has found both.

kidstories

Questions to Consider

1. Ryan was very bothered by stereotypes. He felt it was unfair that people judged him because of his intelligence, the clothes he wore, or the place he lived. What stereotypes do people have about you and your friends? How could you go about trying to change these attitudes?

2. Ryan found many adults in his school who were ready to help him appreciate his talents—classroom teachers, a gifted program teacher, a guidance counselor. Who are the people in your school (and outside of school, too) who always notice your strengths, even when you don't see them yourself? Is there anyone you would like to talk to about a problem in your life, or to thank for helping you through a rough time? If so, make an appointment to talk with them.

Resources

Ryan's life started changing when his teacher made him the director of the Thanksgiving class play. Would you like to try directing or acting? Making costumes or running the lights? Painting scenery? There are many things to do in a play. You may want to get involved at your school. Someday you may want to join the International Thespian Society, an honor society for high school students. For more information, write or call:

> **International Thespian Society**
> **3368 Central Parkway**
> **Cincinnati, OH 45225**
> **(513) 559-1996**

Another important change in Ryan's life was being part of his school's Future Problem Solving Program team. FPSP is an international program for students in grades K-12. Is your school in FPSP? If it is, maybe you can get involved. If it isn't, ask your teacher to write or call for more information:

> **Future Problem Solving Program**
> **115 Main Street, Box 98**
> **Aberdeen, NC 28315**
> **(919) 944-4707**

kidstories

TAKING CHARGE OF YOUR OWN EDUCATION

When schools are good, they are very, very good. But when they are bad, well...you know the rest. For many students, school gives them all the learning options they could ever want or need. Like a feast for the brain, these schools fill the mind and spirit with a steady diet of satisfying courses, served up by expert chefs called teachers. When this happens, everybody wins: kids learn, teachers are fulfilled, and parents vote to increase the school's budget.

Occasionally, though, schools fail, students fail, teachers fail. Nobody is happy when this occurs. Some schools seem a lot like factories, stamping out student after student. They seem most interested in graduating students who are all alike, not unique. How sad.

In the following biographies, you'll read about students who, through hard work and patience, got a good education by working through "the system." You'll also read about one student who had to leave school in order to fully develop his talents.

Just as there is no such thing as "one size fits all" in clothes (despite what the labels might say), there is no school that fits each and every student perfectly. Alterations must be made to accommodate the different and varied types of students. So, the real lessons of these biographies are that education is a two-way street—students learn from teachers, and teachers learn from students. And real learning involves active participation, not passive acceptance.

4

CLEANING UP THE ENVIRONMENT:
The Story of Jennifer Van Vertloo

FAMILY AND BACKGROUND

When Jennifer talks about her town, Edwardsville, Illinois, and her high school, she speaks only in positives and superlatives. "Our city is known for its fine school district. The high school's band and orchestra are top-notch, and our Tigers Baseball Team just won the state championship."

Living with her two younger brothers, parents, and pets (Felix the cat and Herman the dog), Jennifer keeps busy by drawing nature scenes and reading books by many authors, including her favorite, Laura Ingalls Wilder. Also, when she's not attending her ninth-grade classes, 14-year-old Jennifer enjoys biking, swimming, softball, and tennis.

In addition to these typical teenage activities, Jennifer is acutely interested in environmental clean-up.

It all started when she was watching a TV news program. A brief feature story called "50 Things You Can Do to Save the Earth" highlighted simple activities that anyone, even kids, can do to improve the planet's health. While watching this show, Jennifer began to think that she could help promote environmental awareness among her high school classmates. As she put it, "You don't have to be grown-up to do something worthwhile."

Her next step was to try to rally other students around her cause, putting into practice the advice of a popular bumper sticker: "Think globally, act locally."

"I tried to promote environmental awareness by directing my efforts mainly towards an audience of teens," she explains. "So far, in my campaign against 'Planet Destruction,' I have organized a trash pick-up for our social studies class, contacted a speaker who lectured at our school on recycling, and written to several people asking for their support in forming an organization promoting environmental affairs."

By getting herself involved in an endeavor that tuned her in to local environmental problems, Jennifer came to learn a very important truth: that nature is our teacher, not our servant. She also learned something about the connection between attitudes and actions.

"Nowadays," she observes, "a lot of people have negative attitudes. They have no hope or faith in themselves or anyone else. Many of these people just need an optimistic someone to lead the way. By looking on the bright side of things, and by approaching challenges saying 'Yes, I can,' I believe I can get others to feel positive, too."

There were, and continue to be, some problems for Jennifer. For one, the people she wrote to for advice and assistance never wrote back. Since some of these people were community leaders and business owners, Jennifer plans to write follow-up letters, "in case the others got lost in the mail." When the same people get another letter from her, Jennifer believes, they will know she is serious about her campaign.

Also, Jennifer has plans to tell younger students about the importance of recycling and environmental clean-up, as she believes that "some high school students are too caught up in their own lives to care as much as they should about the environment." And Jennifer thinks that once elementary students have the facts about their environment, they'll be willing to help clean up their schools and their neighborhoods.

Lastly, she has asked her physical education teacher to take one day out of his regular schedule to allow students to pick up trash around the school during gym period. "Imagine if *every* phys. ed. teacher did that just once!" she exclaims.

The optimism Jennifer feels for her planet and the people who live on it has its source in her own belief in herself. "I have come to realize that there is no problem that cannot be solved," she says. "If one works hard enough, a solution will be found."

Bolstered by the confidence instilled in her by her parents ("They always listen to my ideas and give their own opinions—I thrive on this input!"), Jennifer knows that she will continue to encourage people to play an active role in securing their planet's health. Once again, it is her attitude that makes her so convincing. "I feel really good," she insists. "I feel like I'm making my life count. I've learned that ignorance and carelessness brought the world down, so now, hard work and dedication are needed to restore it. Progress will be slow, but by giving your all to a cause, a difference *will* be made."

What Jennifer has learned goes beyond the obvious. Sure, she has learned something about environmental issues. But perhaps even more importantly, she has gained a sense of self-respect and confidence. In Jennifer's mind, if she can imagine it, she can do it.

Believing that "it is my destiny to campaign against pollution and planet destruction," Jennifer plans a career involving environmental action. "Someday," she claims, "I would like to start an environmental organization."

At school, Jennifer sees the need to include in the curriculum "more activities that benefit good causes—like cleaning up a park, or helping less fortunate people." She would also like to expand these ideas to her home town ("our neighborhood needs to become more 'neighborly'"), and to the world at large ("people need to open their eyes and acknowledge that the Earth is falling apart"). Jennifer is on a mission: a global journey of hope that will ensure a safer environment for herself and the generations to follow.

And she believes that any changes for the better must begin with the assumption that even kids can make a difference. "If you really believe in a cause, I mean *really* believe in it, then don't just sit back and let it go by; do something about it," she says. "I've also discovered that there are no age limits. Even a five-year-old can accomplish a task of great meaning."

Questions to Consider

1. With Jennifer, there seems to be a link between attitude and accomplishment. Her "I can do it" approach to life has made her feel very secure in trying out new ideas. Think of a time in your own life when your attitude affected your performance, either positively or negatively. Describe this situation, paying special attention to any specific "turning points" that affected your performance.

2. There are environmental causes in every community that need more attention (and money) than they are getting. What are the "hot issues" in your own town (for example, recycling, solid waste disposal, hazardous waste materials, pollution)? Which persons and organizations are working to improve the situation(s)? Are any school-wide organizations set up to explore these concerns? Research these efforts, and select one that is of interest to you and others. Then do what Jennifer did: Take some initial action steps.

Resources

Find out more about what you can do to help your environment. Read *50 Things You Can Do to Save the Earth* (Earthworks Press, 1989) and *The Kid's Guide to Social Action* (Free Spirit Publishing, 1991).

The Kid's Guide to Social Action takes up where *50 Things* leaves off by giving you examples of real changes made by real kids, and step-by-step instructions to help you write effective letters, prepare successful speeches, get media attention, initiate or change laws, and more to make a difference in the world.

The following organizations are good sources of information about the environment. You may even want to join one or more of them.

Cousteau Society
930 W. 21st Street
Norfolk, VA 23517
(804) 627-1144

Greenpeace
1436 U Street, NW
Washington, D.C. 20013
(800) 368-5748

National Wildlife Foundation
1400 16th Street, NW
Washington, D.C. 20036
(800) 432-6564

The U.S. Environmental Protection Agency offers special programs for young people. Have your parents or teachers write or call:

U.S. Environmental Protection Agency
Office of External Relations and Education
Youth Programs (A-108)
401 M Street, SW
Washington, D.C. 20460
(202) 382-4454

5

THE PERFECT EQUATION:
The Story of Christopher Csanady

No matter what type of environment you like (except, maybe, mountains), Chris Csanady is close to it. He lives in Glenview, Illinois, just a few minutes north of downtown Chicago, but since his home borders a forest preserve and is near Lake Michigan, his surroundings offer a lot of diversity ...except in his neighbors.

FAMILY AND
BACKGROUND

"There are no other kids my age nearby," Chris explains. "My neighbors don't even like kids!" Which is unfortunate for them, since 14-year-old Chris shares his home with a younger sister and brother. Also at home are Chris's parents and his golden retriever, C.J. His grandparents live just down the street, which Chris really enjoys, "because having four grown-ups around, there is almost always someone who will say YES!"

A high school freshman, Chris has lived in Glenview all his life. His many interests include mechanized LEGO building, model building, and anything involving problem solving and puzzles. Computer games, outdoor sports (especially tennis), bike riding, and reading scientific magazines and catalogs are among the many other things that Chris enjoys.

MAKING A
DIFFERENCE

One area in which Chris has always excelled is mathematics. He wanted to take algebra in eighth grade, but the principal didn't think he could handle it. So his request was denied.

However, this did not stop Chris from pursuing his mathematical interests. His parents agreed to hire a tutor, a retired math teacher named Mr. Vernoy Johnson, who taught Chris the elements of algebra. Chris liked Mr. Johnson because "it was nice having someone around who would and could answer all my questions in great detail. He was more than a great teacher. He made learning fun, and he answered all my questions even if they weren't about algebra."

Serving as both mentor and teacher, Mr. Johnson helped convince Chris of the extent of his mathematical talents. And, thanks to Betty Meckstroth and Richard Gershon, counselors at nearby Northwestern University, Chris found out about a summer program for students who are especially good in math.

Called the Midwest Talent Search, this program (and others like it throughout the U.S.) serves thousands of junior high students annually who enjoy and excel at math. Chris fit this description. He had taken the Scholastic Aptitude Test (S.A.T.) and scored very well in math.

kidstories

Because of his S.A.T. score, Chris was invited to attend a three-week-long Talent Search program at Northwestern. At first, he was surprised by the invitation. "I never really thought of myself as being gifted," he says. "Neither did my school! But I always knew I was different and better at most tasks than the average person."

He decided to take advantage of this opportunity, and he entered the program eager to learn. At first, he was disappointed. It seemed that all this program offered was "M.O.T.S."—More Of The Same. "I hated having to review algebra again at North-western," Chris remembers. "I already knew a lot of what was being taught. I refused to do my homework because everything was always too easy. I spent a lot of time being angry."

What a bind, and what a letdown. If even a nationally-renowned program at an internationally famous university like Northwestern wasn't challenging enough for Chris, what was wrong?

As it turned out, Chris didn't need a different program. What he needed was a different attitude. His teacher, Don Field, and his dorm counselor, Alf Estberg, spent extra time with Chris, assuring him that there was a purpose behind the review work he was doing. "They made me understand the importance of doing homework," Chris explains. "And they told me that if they didn't care, or if they didn't feel I was worth the effort, they would have given up on me."

By teaching Chris *why* he was learning *what* he was learning, Chris says, "Mr. Field taught me how I could teach myself. Through him, I learned how to learn." And Mr. Estberg gave him homework support. He helped Chris "to understand questions and concepts just by being there and being patient."

For Chris to believe in himself, he needed someone else to believe in him. He found what he needed at North-western, and he is pleased to report that he "mastered Honors Algebra and got a final grade of A minus."

As Chris now recalls his first college experience, he does so with a sense of pride and a positive outlook toward the

LESSONS LEARNED

future. "It felt great!" he says. "My goal was to master algebra and I did it! I also learned some geometry. I also learned that I could take care of myself; I could be responsible. I made lots of friends. For the first time, I wasn't lonely."

What does Chris think of the Talent Search program? "It was an experience not to be forgotten," he exclaims. "I can't wait to go back next summer, and I am now looking forward to going to college."

PERSONAL
GOALS,
GLOBAL
CONCERNS

Because he had such a successful experience at Northwestern, Chris hopes one day to attend the Massachusetts Institute of Technology—M.I.T.—to combine his favorite subjects of math and science, leading (he hopes) to a career in a field such as engineering or design.

Looking back, he would like to see some changes made in the junior high school he attended. First, he'd replace the principal, and next, he'd change the school's gifted program. "It was only for people who got all A's and liked doing homework," he explains. However, he would keep teachers like Ken Koehler and Jane Friesma, both of whom helped Chris understand and pursue his interests in science, computers, and woodshop.

Right now, he's enjoying high school. For him, it's "a big change...new people and more opportunities." Also, Alf Estberg, Chris's dorm counselor from the Talent Search program at Northwestern, was hired recently at Chris's high school. "He still acts as a mentor and friend," Chris says. "It's great to see him every day."

Looking toward the future, Chris would like to see a world without weapons. "I would make a new justice system, and I would have one world government so that there would not be war," he says. "And I would undo the Greenhouse Effect and look for peaceful solutions to the world's problems."

In closing, Chris acknowledges two people who helped him see that he was not the only person in the world whose talents exceeded what his school was willing to offer him. First, there was Betty Meckstroth, who was "the first person who started me

kidstories

believing in myself. She helped me to learn that there are other kids who feel like I do."

Who was the other person who helped him to appreciate his talents? Himself. "I learned that you can do whatever it is you are striving for," Chris says. "Most of all, believe in yourself."

Questions to Consider

1. School rules and attitudes prevented Chris from taking the academic challenges he was ready for. He succeeded in accomplishing his self-set goals, but he did so in spite of school rather than because of it. Are there any rules in your school, written or unwritten, that could prevent students from progressing academically? If so, select one that especially bothers you and ask a teacher, principal, or counselor how you might go about changing this policy.

2. Chris emphasizes the importance of doing homework. What are your feelings about the homework you are assigned? Is some homework more worthwhile than other homework? Describe and discuss homework assignments that are especially good, and those that are especially bad.

Resources

Chris learned a lot about math, and about himself, because of the Midwest Talent Search program. Talent Searches across the country identify high achievers at the middle school level by analyzing standardized achievement test scores, like the S.A.T. Then they give suggestions about how students can use and develop their talents. They charge a fee for their services. You may want to contact the Talent Search in your area.

Center for Talent Development
Midwest Talent Search
Northwestern University
2003 Sheridan Road
Evanston, IL 60208
(708) 491-3711

C.T.Y.
Johns Hopkins University
3400 North Charles Street
Baltimore, MD 21218
(301) 338-8427

Duke Talent Identification Program
Duke University
P.O. Box 40077
Durham, NC 27706
(919) 684-3847

Rocky Mountain Talent Search
University of Denver
Margery Reed Hall 114
Denver, CO 80208
(303) 871-2533

Center for Study of Capable Youth
University of Washington
Guthrie Annex II, NI-20
Seattle, WA 98195
(206) 543-4160

Center for Academic Precocity
Arizona State University
Farmer Building 417
Tempe, AZ 85287
(602) 965-4754

Chris had a "college experience" while he was in junior high school. Do you know that you can earn *college credit* as early as high school? Advanced Placement (A.P.) classes are college-level courses taught in many high schools. Successfully completing a course and its exam qualifies you for college credit. There's a free booklet, "Guide to the Advanced Placement Program," that can tell you more. To request a copy, write to:

College Board Publication Orders
Box 886
New York, NY 10101

6

THE HEART OF A WRITER:
The Story of Jerry Simmons

Often schools succeed, but sometimes they don't. Maybe it isn't anything in particular that turns students off to their school experiences, but for a variety of reasons, kids, teachers, and course work can misconnect. Such was the case with Jerry Simmons.

FAMILY AND BACKGROUND

Jerry is a 17-year-old college student from San Jose, California. He didn't get to college in the usual way. In his junior year, Jerry withdrew from the typical high school in which he was enrolled and entered the Independent Studies Program (ISP) sponsored by his school district.

In ISP, Jerry explains, students "come in once a week for an hour and turn in the work that they were assigned the previous week." Recently, Jerry passed the California Proficiency Test, qualifying him for his high school diploma. He's now attending a nearby junior college.

Jerry lives with his mom and visits with his dad one day each week. His grandmother "lives about two miles away, and since she is around the house a lot, she's part of the family." Jerry has two older brothers, both married; Mark is 27 and a college pastor, and Brian is 25 and is studying to become a missionary. Also sharing Jerry's household are three pets—Pookie, a bird; Happy, a dog; and a nameless desert tortoise.

Jerry's interests and hobbies include hybridizing and growing irises, clogging (a type of folk dancing), church activities, and genealogy (the study of family trees).

MAKING A DiFFERENCE

Since Jerry chose to leave high school as soon as he could, you might wonder if he ever liked or succeeded in school. The answer is yes on both counts.

For example, Jerry has enjoyed writing since he was very young. *The Mouse and the Genius*, a book he wrote as a fourth grader, won a certificate of merit at a local conference for young authors. Later, in eighth grade, Jerry's story on the dangers of smoking won a school award. "Each time I wrote," Jerry explains, "I was encouraged to do more, better."

Then came high school. And, as Jerry remembers, "a bomb-shell hit." Up until then, he had received awards and recognition for his writing. Now "a high school teacher told me that she *hated* my writing. Not just the content, but the style, *everything*!"

This confused Jerry, as he had received praise from dozens of other teachers about the quality of his work. Successful poets and other writers who taught mini-courses in Jerry's school had chosen his work "out of stacks of others" to read to the class.

As a result of this unsettling experience with his writing teacher, and several other problems with what he calls "very restrictive policies," Jerry began searching in his sophomore year for an alternative high school program. He wanted something better suited to his independent learning preferences; something that would help him achieve his self-set goals. It took a while, but he finally found ISP.

Meanwhile, Jerry's dad bought him a book on free-lance writing, and Jerry became inspired. "The book said to write about what you know—which, in my case, was irises," he says. "My family has been growing them since before I was born; I guess I learned all about them through osmosis! So I wrote an article on irises for my local newspaper, and it was rejected. Then I wrote a similar article with a different focus and it got published."

This initial success gave Jerry the confidence to write more articles for other newspapers and magazines. He has since written articles and feature columns for regional, national, and international publications, including *Southern Star*, a notable Russian journal published in English.

"It's truly an accomplishment to have published so much already," he admits. "I'm pleased with myself because I've defied all the odds. Editors are now calling me with ideas rather than my having to write letters to them."

Also, Jerry recently submitted his first book proposal to a publisher, which is rare for someone not even old enough to sign a legal contract. "Now I know," he says, "that I must have talent, or I wouldn't have gotten anywhere near this far."

F or Jerry, high school was a roller-coaster ride that resulted in a slew of mixed emotions about the role adults have played in his life. What got him through the rough spots was persistence and a feeling that things would eventually work out. He trusted that "sooner or later I'd find a market for my ideas, and sooner or later I'd find editors I felt comfortable dealing with, who would pass a good word about me to other editors."

LESSONS
LEARNED

Jerry is especially grateful to those editors and authors who took the time to respond to his ideas, and for the support of his parents both before and during ISP. His mom and dad both reassured Jerry that his dreams were realistic. Jerry also credits a mightier power for his success: "I feel it is God's will that has allowed so many things to fall into line at the same time."

Personal achievements and encouragement from others increased Jerry's self-confidence in both the field of writing and the field of living. "Most of all," he says, "I learned that there is great strength inside all of us which can be realized if we set definite goals and go after them. For example, conducting interviews seems very easy now, but I would have been terrified if I had to do that even just a few years ago."

With the support of parents, poets, and professional editors, and an inner strength and belief in his own talents and a power greater than his own, Jerry Simmons continues to make a difference in the world of writing. And it all began in fourth grade with *The Mouse and the Genius*.

PERSONAL GOALS, GLOBAL CONCERNS

Just as Jerry's writing interests are varied, so are the career choices he is considering. Some possibilities are politics, history, library science, law, entrepreneurship, diplomacy, teaching, marketing, psychology, and journalism. Since selecting just one of these options might be too difficult to do, Jerry has considered creating a career instead of merely picking one that already exists. "I hope," he says, "to find a career where some elements of many of the above occupations will be needed. That would be truly rewarding."

Where school is concerned, given the chance, Jerry would reform education by guaranteeing students' rights, including an uncensored student press. Classes, too, could be improved by "teaching more than just dates and places...and having lots of creative opportunities in regular classes, like writing, painting, and dance."

Relying once more on the power of words, Jerry would like to see them used to promote global understanding. "I believe that the pen *is* mightier than the sword," he says, "and that written language should be used more aggressively to vent emotions, rather than using weapons."

That's precisely what good writers have been doing for centuries—writers with the passion of Jerry Simmons.

Questions to Consider

1. Although he had many teachers who recognized his writing talents, Jerry seemed most affected by the one teacher who *did not* like his work. Why do you think Jerry concentrated so much on this one person's opinion rather than the many people who appreciated his work? Have you ever had a teacher who affected you in a negative way? What did that person say or do, and how did it change your attitude or your work habits?

2. The Independent Studies Program in which Jerry enrolled seemed to be a good alternative for him. Would you like to participate in such a program? What do you think its benefits and drawbacks might be? Investigate any alternatives to the typical high school placement that exist in your school district, and discover the reasons that students have selected these various options.

Resources

Jerry became inspired when his dad bought him a book on free-lance writing. You may want to visit your local library and scan the shelves for books on this subject. Jerry recommends *Freelance Writing for Magazines and Newspapers* by Marcia Yudkin (Harper & Row, 1988), but you're sure to find many others as well.

Some publishers accept children's writing, but most do not. Jerry decided that as long as he was knowledgeable about his subject, it was not necessary to reveal how old he was. "I have never met any of my editors," he says, "so my writing is judged solely on its own merits, and there is no discrimination because of my age."

When he wanted to find out about free-lance writing, he turned to books and magazines written for adults. There is one he considers "essential": *Writer's Market* (Writer's Digest Books, updated annually). This directory lists thousands of places that buy articles, books, jokes, greeting cards, short stories, and more from free-lance writers. It also includes articles of interest to free-lance writers. You'll find a copy in your library's reference section.

---

kidstories

Writer's Digest and *The Writer* are magazines about writing and publishing. Many libraries subscribe to one or both of these. If your library doesn't, write or call:

Writer's Digest
Box 2123
Harlan, IA 50593
(800) 333-0133

The Writer
The Writer, Inc.
120 Boylston Street
Boston, MA 02116
(617) 423-3157

If you're not quite ready to tackle the grown-up writer's market, that's okay. There are books that tell you about publishers (and contests) that especially want writing by young people. Read about these on page 72.

7

AIMING FOR THE STARS:
The Story of
Mark Anthony McKibben

Mark calls himself "an only child in a family of four," which tells you something about the prominent place that Dixie, his dog, holds in the family hierarchy. A 17-year-old high school senior at Trinity High School in Garfield Heights, Ohio, Mark lives in a "not very exclusive area, but it's where my whole life began."

FAMILY AND BACKGROUND

Mark transferred into Trinity from a different Catholic school, after being disappointed that its renowned "high standards" applied only to certain things, "basically football and baseball." At Trinity, Mark found "a sense of well-rounded tradition and a friendly environment." To him, it is a place to grow and learn.

In naming his interests, Mark describes them as "eccentric" (unusual), but a better description might be "eclectic" (varied). For instance, he enjoys tennis and bowling, working on computers and watching movies—especially comedy and horror films.

He also believes strongly in the importance of a social life. "If you don't mingle with others," he explains, "you get brain-fried."

MAKING A DIFFERENCE

In addition to these many interests, Mark enjoys studying about space exploration. In both the eighth and ninth grades, he spent a week at Space Camp in Huntsville, Alabama, where (among other activities) he was able to fly a plane and pilot a shuttle mission in a flight simulator.

It was at Space Camp that Mark learned about an ongoing project called Students for the Exploration and Development of Space (SEDS). In SEDS, students are invited to submit project proposals for scientific experiments they would like to see conducted in space. Armed with the proposal guidelines and an idea for a possible experiment, Mark headed home to Garfield Heights to complete his application.

"I submitted an experiment for a project entitled 'Germination of Various Seed Types in a Micro-gravity Environment' when I was 14," Mark explains. "Approximately one month later, I received an acceptance letter from NASA [National Aeronautics and Space Administration], along with the names of three other students. Together, we would have to compile a project that would eventually fly on a shuttle mission."

Initial excitement gave way to stark reality when Mark learned that his three "lab partners" were from various regions of the United States. "We could never meet each other, we lived so far apart," he says. "One student was from Maryland, another from Kansas, and another from Illinois. We were grouped together because of the similarity of our project ideas."

kidstories

Using the telephone and the postal service, these four young scientists began to communicate their ideas about how they might conduct their space experiment. Still, for Mark, something was missing. He wanted daily contact with others who could help him refine his ideas and test out his experiments. So, two years ago, he assembled a team of five other Trinity students to help him with his ground experiments.

For a while, those students, along with a Trinity faculty adviser, helped Mark to gather data on seed and bean germination that will be used in putting the finishing touches on his space-bound experiment. It is scheduled to go up on a shuttle mission within the next two years.

Recently Mark traveled to the Marshall Space Flight Center in Huntsville to meet the other three students with whom he has been working, long-distance, for over three years. There they combined their efforts and results to prepare a seed canister that will travel into space. Also, this scientific team got to meet with space science engineers from the University of Alabama, who gave Mark and his teammates more suggestions for improving their experiment.

W hen this project is finally completed, Mark will have spent more than half of his teenage years working on the same assignment. This long-term commitment in itself should be a source of pride, and it is. But Mark has even more reasons to feel good about himself and his efforts.

LESSONS LEARNED

Along the way, he has encountered roadblocks, both scientific and personal. "We had problems with basic scientific experimentation," Mark remembers. "That is always to be expected, and you leave room for errors and bad conclusions. We overcame that problem by simply fixing and changing the variables, and experimenting more and more and more!"

Another problem was not so easily overcome: the disunity in the group at Trinity. "Things became very hectic and we began to resent each other," Mark says. "We were crabby all the time and we went downhill."

After four months of intense work, the team decided to break up. Once more, Mark was "on his own," working to finish what he had started one-and-one-half years before.

Interestingly, he doesn't resent the fact that the Trinity group split up. In fact, he sees the whole series of incidents related to this project as a learning experience. "It really helped me to gain necessary confidence," he says, "and at the same time, it has helped me to experience failure, both in the experiment and in the split-up of the group. So, I've learned how to cope with errors, and I also believe that I've built some character."

Meeting his long-distance project partners helped Mark to get excited again about the possibilities of their experiment. Although each student had to pay for transportation to and from Huntsville, NASA paid for their meals and lodging. NASA has also spent more than $10,000 to purchase the "Getaway Canister" that will contain the seeds in this space-bound experiment.

Mark and his colleagues still have to raise at least $10,000 more to pay for other materials—neoprene balloons, aluminum shielding, the seeds, the computer processing unit for the canister, and so on. "I hope to convince some local corporations to donate some money, and thereby become sponsors of this experiment," Mark says.

Raising this money may seem an impossible task, but Mark sees it as merely one more hurdle to overcome on the road to success. And he offers this encouragement to anyone who would like to follow his lead: "My advice to prospective students who want to go into large-scale experimentation would be to remain calm and patient. Things are not always going to turn out as you expect—in fact, they seldom do! But don't let that discourage you. Keep on experimenting, be yourself, and be open with your team members. Then success will be yours."

When kids are little, they want to grow up to be all sorts of exotic adventurers: professional athletes, actors, lion tamers, astronauts. Some manage to hold onto those goals and achieve them. That is Mark's ambition.

"I really hope to work as either a mathematician or an astrophysicist for NASA," he says. "However, my ultimate goal is to become an astronaut. I really can't explain why these fields interest me so much, other than I really like the satisfaction of solving problems."

There are other problems to solve in this world, Mark knows. One way to begin on a global scale is to "rid the world of corrupt officials and ignorant leaders." From this would follow a cleaner, greener Earth; world unity; and fewer problems with some of "our collective worst enemies—nuclear weapons, pollution, and drug abuse."

Mark's NASA project will allow him to see his work reach heights (literally!) seldom achieved by high school students. True to the mission of the space shuttle program, Mark is proving that the dream is still alive.

Questions to Consider

1. Mark was confronted with many difficulties during his NASA project—failed experiments, long-distance team members, the split-up of his Trinity group, and the simple fact that his project has (so far) taken over three years. What do you think kept him going during these problem stages? Why didn't he just give up and move on to another topic or project? Now consider your own life. Have you ever been involved in a project that took you a year or longer to complete? Describe it, and the ups and downs you faced along the way.

2. Murphy's Law states (in part): "If something can go wrong, it will go wrong." Mark certainly found Murphy's Law to be true for his project. What projects have you been involved with that had their share of problems? How did you approach these difficulties, and what was the end result? What have your own experiences with problems taught you about the role mistakes play in everyday life?

Resources

Mark went to Space Camp twice. Space Camp, associated with NASA, is a one-week program where kids in grades 4 and up build rockets and space stations, take part in flight simulations, and learn about space. To find out more, write or call:

Space Camp
Tranquility Base
Huntsville, AL 35805
(205) 837-3413

At Space Camp, Mark found out about the SEDS (Students for the Exploration and Development of Space) project that got him started on his experiment. The goal of SEDS is to implement educational programs that give young people direct experience with space. If you have an idea for a space experiment, write or call:

SEDS
MIT Building W20-445
77 Massachusetts Avenue
Cambridge, MA 02139
(617) 253-8897

NASA also sponsors projects that involve kids. To find out more, write or call:

NASA
Educational Affairs Division
Code FE
400 Maryland Avenue
Washington, D.C. 20546
(202) 453-1110

If you would like to read more about what is happening in space, check out the Smithsonian-sponsored magazine, *Air and Space*. Look for it at your local library, or write or call:

> **AIR AND SPACE Smithsonian**
> **AIAA Building**
> **370 L'Enfant Promenade SW, 10th Floor**
> **Washington, D.C. 20024-2518**
> **(202) 287-2518**

For many people, thinking about the space program reminds them of the *Challenger* disaster of 1986, in which all seven people aboard were killed. If you want to learn more about this event and how it has affected the space program, look for these books in your library:

"I Touch the Future...": The Story of Christa McAuliffe by Robert T. Hohler (Random House, 1986). This book tells the story of the teacher who was one of the passengers on the fatal *Challenger* mission.

Challenger: The Final Voyage by Richard S. Lewis (Columbia University Press, 1988) is full of interesting information about the mission.

The U.S. Space Program After Challenger: Where Are We Going? by Alan Stern (Franklin Watts, 1987) discusses how the *Challenger* disaster is affecting the future of the space program.

8

OUT FRONT AND SHINING:
The Story of Natalie Phillips

Colonial Williamsburg, Busch Gardens, the Wright Brothers Memorial, and Norfolk Naval Base: these are places that serve as exciting diversions for Natalie Phillips, who lives in Virginia Beach, Virginia.

A 13-year-old who attends Kempsville Junior High School,

Natalie lives with her mom and two pets—Sweetie, her tabby cat, and Yentl, her Boston-Scottie. Her grandmother, "Gammy," lives with them "two or three months at a time. She only goes home to check the house in Ohio and get organized so she can hurry back to our more moderate climate."

Also, since Natalie lives in a resort community, "my home life is almost crazy with all the people who come to stay with us. People just pop in and stay for a few days." Natalie enjoys this, though, because it gives her a chance to meet again with relatives and friends whose homes are far away from Virginia Beach.

Natalie likes both her school and her neighborhood, and takes full advantage of the best that each has to offer. At school, she's involved in debate, drama, sports, and academically challenging classes; in her spare time, she enjoys reading, dance, water skiing, piano—even sky diving.

"But," she adds, "before I would do anything else, I'd love to go write something. Writing is my most favorite hobby in the world."

MAKING A DIFFERENCE

When she moved to Virginia three years ago, Natalie began exploring the many activities and events that take place in and around Virginia Beach. One that caught her attention almost immediately was the Miss Virginia Pre-Teen competition. Natalie is the first to stress that this is not just a beauty contest; in fact, the specific contest she entered was the talent competition.

Given Natalie's many interests and talents, it took her a little while to determine what exactly she would perform. But with the help of her piano teacher, Carol Noona, and the encouragement of her mom, Natalie chose to play Friedrich Kuhlau's *Sonatina Opus 55, No. 1*.

"For approximately seven months, I prepared this piece," she explains. "In those seven months I had to cut the performance time from four minutes to two, memorize it completely, and ensure that it would be perfect."

When the day for her performance finally arrived, Natalie learned that there were 127 contestants in the talent category. But her hard work and perseverance paid off, and Natalie found herself among the top four finalists.

What happened next? As Natalie tells it, "On Sunday, June 3 (my birthday!), I played my piece for the second time in front of the judges—and won! I was now Miss Virginia Pre-Teen Talent, and I received a large trophy and a check for $300....When I heard my name called, I was happier than if I had won the overall competition for Miss Virginia Pre-Teen."

A s Natalie reflects on the time and energy she spent on this two-minute recital, she realizes that she has learned an important life lesson. "Now I see that if you work hard at anything you do," she says, "the reward comes back in vast numbers—like $300 worth of numbers!"

Even more important than the cash was her sense of personal accomplishment, for, since winning this competition, Natalie has gone on to other achievements. She attended a string quartet clinic at James Madison University. She student-directed a community theater production, and performed in "Annie" and "Fiddler on the Roof." (In "Fiddler on the Roof," she played both the fiddler and one of his daughters.) And she was the only junior high age student selected to attend a debate clinic at Virginia Wesleyan University.

Any student could be proud of this list of victories. For Natalie, they are especially noteworthy. As she reports, "I was born with a severe hiatal hernia, which means that my intestines had ruptured through my diaphragm. There was only a 20 percent chance that I would live, and even if I did, it was likely I'd be blind, retarded, or need a lot of corrective surgery."

Following an initial operation, infant Natalie was placed on a respirator to help her breathe. After two weeks of touch-and-go, during which she was clinically dead three times, Natalie began breathing on her own. When she finally left the hospital, she did so with "only a large heart murmur and some pretty nasty scars across my stomach. Still, my family was thrilled to have me alive, whatever the later consequences might be."

From that point on, it was all uphill. As Natalie's heart murmur grew less serious—it doesn't affect her at all anymore—she began exploring her world fully. She learned to swim at 11 months ("good therapy for my lungs"). She played Bach and Mozart on piano and violin by age five, and she has learned to speak Hebrew, Chinese, and Russian. As Natalie states, "'Out Front and Shining,' that's my mom's motto for me."

Throughout her life, Natalie has received strong support from her extended family. "They encouraged me and tried to relieve the pressure of everyday life," she says. And even though she was too young to remember her ordeal as a baby, Natalie still "appreciates the intense love and prayer that they have surrounded me with my whole life."

What advice would she give to other students on how best to use their abilities? "If you can play an instrument," she recommends, "do something special with it. It's a gift; it's your talent. Don't be afraid or shy to play somewhere if you're asked, because you'll become special to others for sharing your talents with them."

PERSONAL GOALS, GLOBAL CONCERNS

Sharing and caring are very important to Natalie, and she wishes that people in her school would show more concern for themselves and others. "Teachers and other adults should foster in kids the importance of self-esteem," she says. "Kids who are 'grits' or 'hoods' are thought of as immature and uneducated, and therefore they develop low self-esteem, which is caused by criticism. In order to bring students together, teachers should place a greater emphasis on discussion."

Natalie's wish for better human relations has led her to consider a career in psychology "because people need help coping with their problems." However, she is also considering other options, including business administration and writing. Her ideal career would be as a film writer, and she would like to know enough about psychology to help herself "understand and get beyond writer's block."

kidstories

Natalie's concern for self-esteem even includes world affairs. As she explains, "This world can mean so much more only if people would care, like I do, to save not only my country, but the countries of the world that make up this beautiful planet."

Through good times and bad, Natalie remains optimistic. Thanks to the support of many family members who have shown her that good things can happen when you believe they will, she is sure to remain "out front and shining."

Questions to Consider

1. Some people dislike the idea of pageants like the Miss Virginia Pre-Teen competition, arguing that they are nothing more than beauty contests. These same people might say that these contests exploit people, since they emphasize looks over talent or intelligence. What is your view on competitions like the one in which Natalie took part? Why do you feel the way you do?

2. Natalie's mother has allowed and encouraged Natalie to take part in many physical activities including swimming, sky diving, and water skiing. How do you think this has affected Natalie's attitudes about life? If *you* were Natalie's parent, would you let her try such strenuous sports, or would you prefer that she participate in less physically demanding activities?

Resources

Can you imagine what it would be like to be born with a health problem, like Natalie was, or to develop one later in life? One way to find out is by reading books about kids with disabilities. Look for these at your library, and ask your librarian for other recommendations:

What If You Couldn't...? by Janet Kemien (Scribners, 1979) gives you some idea what it's like to have seeing, hearing, learning, and physical problems.

Like It Is: Facts and Feelings about Handicaps from Kids Who Know by Barbara Adams (Walker & Co., 1979) gives kids' perspectives on their own disabilities.

9

POETIC JUSTICE:
The Story of
Kerry Thompson

Just down the
road from
pineapple farms,
amidst acres of
tropical fruits,
lies the rural
community of
Caboolture—Aboriginal
for "home of the carpet
snake." It is here that
eight-year-old Kerry
Thompson calls home.

You'll find Cabool-
ture in Australia, in the
state of Queensland, 25

miles north of the state capital of Brisbane. (Like the U.S., Australia is divided into states.)

Kerry attends Caboolture State Primary School, which has over 1,000 students and is one of the largest primary schools in the state. ("Primary" schools in Australia are similar to K-8 elementary schools in the U.S.) She lives on a small farm with her parents, and though she is an only child, Kerry shares the land with a variety of pets: a dog, a cat, mice, parrots, chickens, a duck, and a Clydesdale horse named Rose.

Also, she spends a lot of time with her neighbor, a person Kerry describes as "a voluntary wildlife care person who tends to the needs of injured kangaroos and kooka-burras."

As is obvious, Kerry is fond of animals, "but my greatest love is horses and anything to do with horses." She also enjoys producing hand-built or wheel-thrown pottery, performing music ("I love to play for the elderly people in nursing homes"), and conducting all types of hands-on science experiments.

And she has another talent besides: Kerry is a poet.

MAKING A DIFFERENCE

Nothing!
Not one color to be seen
Just a grayish sheen
Until...
Softly, the arch of a rainbow appeared
Dancing in the shadows of the grey nothing world.
The rainbow dropped its colours on all things alive
Every colour that it painted helps us to survive.

So begins one of Kerry's original poems, *Colours*, a tribute to the rainbow and the pieces of nature that share its "colours"— like a "tabby cat," "rusty things," and "green apple cider."

Kerry's first poem appeared in print when she was five-and-one-half years old. It was published in a nationwide literary magazine, *Scope*, produced by The Fellowship of Australian Writers. Since then, she has won many awards for her poems. "I even presented one of my poems to the Premier of Queensland, at Parliament House," she says proudly. This would

kidstories

be similar to performing for the President of the United States in Washington, D.C., or Canada's Prime Minister in Ottawa, Ontario.

Recently Kerry had the privilege of meeting one of her favorite British authors, Pam Ayres, who writes children's books. The two of them discussed Kerry's writing, as well as a problem that has plagued Kerry several times since she started entering writing contests. As Kerry explains, "When I enter a competition for children of my own age, I rarely win. I think the judges think that I didn't do the work."

What the judges don't know is that Kerry has been reading since she was two years old. She even attended a "writer's camp" on three weekends at the Brisbane College of Advanced Education when she was five, and she has been writing poems on a regular basis since then.

Her next goal? "To fill a 48-page botany book with 24 poems and illustrations and have this published," she says. "So far, I've finished 14 pages."

Due to the efforts of a man named Ralph Pirozzo, who directs a statewide activity program called the Peninsula Enrichment Program for Gifted and Talented (PEP), Kerry has been able to participate in many events that spotlighted her writing talents. Over the past ten years, thousands of children have participated in PEP, including many from economically disadvantaged or geographically isolated regions of Queensland.

Thanks to PEP, and to the many opportunities it has given Kerry to develop her writing talents, she says she is "happy, excited, and proud." And even though she has not won every competition she has entered, Kerry does feel that a writer needs to have "self-confidence and persistence. These will go a long way in achieving almost anything you want to do." She advises other young people to "read all you can on your subject and listen to those who are experts in their fields."

LESSONS LEARNED

At school, Kerry feels the need for additional challenges. "The biggest problem for me is trying not to be bored," she explains. "Our school system caters to the average child, but is hopeless when it comes to brighter children. I would change the system so that all children are taught at a level that is suitable to their understanding, not a system graded on age."

As a child with multiple and varied interests, Kerry is considering several possible careers including music or science. She likes music "because it can be enjoyed by almost everybody," and science "because it is our future, for better or worse." Kerry would also like to teach children to care for and ride horses.

Her interest in science and nature extends into her dreams for the land "down under" and the planet we all share. "I would plant more trees to replace the rain forests that have been destroyed," she says, "and encourage people to use solar power for heating and electricity. Here in Australia, the sun shines every day of the year! Also, I would ban all chemicals that damage the ozone layer, and refuse to allow imports of rain forest timber."

Kerry Thompson is a young girl who sees life around her, appreciates it, and chronicles its beauty for others to enjoy. This eight-year-old from Queensland has many wonderful gifts. See how she describes a turtle-hatching area near her home:

The Moonlight March at Mon Repos

It's just gone dusk,
The waves roll in at Mon Repos.
We sit on the sand and wait to catch a glimpse
of the Gentle Giants of the deep.
We look around, we're not alone,
Many more have come to see
The gentle giants of the sea.
Hush! says one, there's movement on the shore,
There is, cries one—No—It's a rock, says another,
If it's a rock it's moving, says another
No lights please, says Ranger Tom,
or she won't be back tonight.

Up the dunes, here comes,
stand back give her space, says Ranger Tom.
We all stand still and watch as the Gentle Giant Turtle
digs her nest and lays her eggs.
We stand and watch her leave the sands of Mon Repos
But we'll be back in two months time
To catch a glimpse of the Hatchlings
in their Moonlight March at Mon Repos.

Kerry Thompson
Age 8

Questions to Consider

1. Kerry seems to have many obvious talents, yet she still complains that school is unrewarding for her. If you were one of Kerry's teachers, what might you suggest she do in school to make it more interesting and worthwhile?

2. Children's author Pam Ayres is one of Kerry's heroes, and the two of them got together to talk about their mutual interests—a very exciting and special moment in Kerry's young life. If you were to select one famous person to meet and talk with, who would it be, and what would you talk about? Why would you choose this person over all others?

Resources

The PEP program Kerry is involved in was started in 1979 by Ralph Pirozzo, an Australian teacher. PEP's main purpose is to organize out-of-school enrichment and extension activities for gifted and talented students and their families. (Mr. Pirozzo believes that the program shouldn't have to depend on the educational system for funding, and that gifted and talented young people shouldn't be off in a group by themselves.) If you want to know more about PEP and other international programs for gifted and talented kids, write to:

> **World Council on Gifted and Talented Children**
> **c/o Norah Maier, Ph.D.**
> **University of Toronto, Faculty of Education**
> **UTS, 371 Bloor Street West**
> **Toronto, Ontario, Canada M5S 2R7**

Are you a writer, like Kerry? Would you like to try getting some of your writing published? Check out the *Market Guide for Young Writers*, edited by Kathy Henderson (Shoe Tree Press, 1990). Revised and updated often, this book lists publications that accept work from young writers, plus writing contests you can enter.

All the Best Contests for Kids by Joan M. Bergstrom and Craig Bergstrom (Ten Speed Press, 1988) also lists many writing contests you can enter.

Would you like to be a better writer? *The Young Writer's Handbook* by Susan J. Tchudi and Stephen Tchudi (Macmillan, 1987) is full of helpful information, from how to write a school report to how to start publishing your writing.

WHEN THE GOING GETS TOUGH

L ife isn't always easy or fair, and things don't always turn out the way we plan. Given these realities, we still all go along as best we can, hoping to make the right decisions at the right times. And with the help of our parents, teachers, friends, and others, we often achieve our goals.

For some kids, however, the path to success is difficult. These kids are as human as anyone—sensitive, caring, capable—but due to life conditions beyond their control, they have to try harder to succeed, or try in different ways.

Sometimes these life conditions are built in, like a physical disability or a learning disability. Sometimes they are geographical or cultural, like when you grow up in a place where you're the only kid in the neighborhood, or you get transplanted to a country where you don't know the language or the customs.

But even these challenges can be met and overcome, as you'll discover in the stories that follow. Each individual highlighted in this section proves the old adage true: "When the going gets tough, the tough get going!"

10

A CREATIVE CHILD WITH A DIFFERENCE:
The Story of Chad Knauer

Chad is a 12-year-old Ohio resident living in the town of Huron, a small city on big Lake Erie. His house has a swimming pool and five occupants Chad describes as "a sister afraid of spiders, a dog afraid of cats, a hamster afraid of me, a father afraid of nothing, and a mother afraid of everything."

FAMILY AND BACKGROUND

Chad's imagination is quite active, and it shows up in his hobbies and interests. He enjoys drawing comics with characters he has invented, and he is always building things in his basement. (One current project is a cardboard city.) He collects foreign and American coins and comic books. "Also," Chad adds, "I enjoy taking occasional trips to Mars."

MAKING A DIFFERENCE

People have been noticing Chad's imagination for quite some time. For example, at age five, he was invited to share his knowledge of dinosaurs with a fifth-grade science class. He gave a lecture and showed some of his drawings to a room full of ten-year-olds.

When Chad started school full time, he began to see everything there as a creative experience ready to be explored. He recalls that he once looked at some cracks in the plaster of his classroom and transformed them, mentally, into a mountain path. He "strolled" down this path until his teacher reminded him of where he was.

Also, when Chad does math, he sees more than just a column of numbers. Each problem takes on a life of its own. Here is what Chad sees when he computes 723 x 35:

kidstories

You may be wondering if Chad's creative talents ever get in the way of his lessons. The answer is yes. As Chad says, "I have trouble keeping up with my class, but my head is full of wonderful things that I want to do and learn."

Why would someone as intelligent and imaginative as Chad have trouble keeping up with his class? Because he has a learning disability. Fortunately, his parents and teachers found out about it when Chad was younger, and they have been able to give him special help.

There are many different kinds of learning disabilities. Chad's has to do with reading and writing. He has trouble deciphering what he tries to read, and it is hard for him to write down his ideas so others can understand them.

Now that he has spent some time in classes for kids with learning disabilities, Chad has learned more about himself. He knows why he is better at some things than others. He knows that having a learning disability doesn't mean you are stupid. His teachers have helped him to organize his schoolwork so that he can be successful.

But there are still some issues that need resolving. As Chad tells it, "The biggest problem I have are some teachers who don't understand that when they ask a question, many answers come to my mind, not just the one they expect. Being identified as a person with a learning disability has helped some, but my parents still have to go to school a lot and remind my teachers that I *do* have a disability, even though they can't see it. They have to keep telling my teachers that I do need to use computers, tape recorders, and so on to learn."

One of the people who kept Chad's creative spark alive in school was his fourth- and fifth-grade teacher, Kathy Hammond. While listening to a lecture on how to recognize creative students, Ms. Hammond kept hearing words like "daydreamer," "turns in assignments late," "disorganized, but lots of ideas." They all reminded her of Chad. To her, Chad was someone who could "come up with ideas very quickly, but who could never find his pencil or his book."

Ms. Hammond decided to have Chad take a special test

called the Torrance Test of Creative Thinking. For this test, Chad was required to create pictures from various lines and squiggles. What happened was very interesting. Chad got the highest possible score. He ended up in the top one percent of everyone who had ever taken the test!

Chad, his parents, and Ms. Hammond were all excited about these results. The testing center that scored his test was so impressed that they offered to provide Chad with two "mentors"—adults who could help Chad further develop his strong creative talents.

The mentors they chose for Chad were Sid and Bea Parnes, world-famous researchers on creativity. When the Parneses learned about Chad, they invited him and his family to visit them at their home in Buffalo, New York.

Chad had a wonderful time. "Sid listened to what I said," he remembers. "He looked at some of the comic books I have drawn, and we did creative problem-solving together in the living room of his home to work on some of my school problems. I hope to go to a creativity camp next summer and meet other kids like me. At least I know what I am now, and why I have all these 'crazy' ideas, and why written work is so hard for me."

The Parneses were impressed with Chad. Sid describes him as "a delightful chap, full of ideas."

LESSONS LEARNED

Though he is still struggling with his learning disability in school, Chad has learned that he can continue exploring and enjoying his many creative abilities. He even feels confident enough to give advice to others.

"If you feel you are different from other kids," he says, "maybe you are, but that is not always bad. Maybe you have a gift of seeing this world in a different way than they do. If you believe you do have talent, go to your parents or anyone in your school who understands creativity and tell them how you feel."

Chad's continuing relationship with Sid and Bea Parnes has helped him to understand and appreciate his own special talents. He is also very thankful to his teacher, Ms. Hammond. Because she went to a lecture on creativity, and because she listened

kidstories

closely, "she realized that the instructor was talking about kids like me."

Using his current interest in drawing as a base for his future ambitions, Chad hopes to become a cartoonist or an animator. (He's already made animated movies with his family's video camera, using clay and toys.) "But," he says, "I'm not sure what I'll end up doing. All I know is that it won't be a desk job—I will be doing something fun!"

When it comes to improving his world, Chad reports that he wants "what everyone else would like: world peace, no wars, no drugs, fast food that doesn't taste like sewage waste, and for people to understand everyone else."

Thanks to people like Ms. Hammond and the Parneses, Chad's goal of understanding has already become a reality for him.

Questions to Consider

1. Millions of people—kids and adults—have some form of learning disability. Maybe, like Chad, they have trouble writing, or reading, or listening to instructions. If there is an LD specialist in your school, ask that person to visit your classroom and talk about learning disabilities. Maybe it will help you and your classmates to better understand that people with a learning disability aren't "dumb."

2. Chad seemed to gain a lot of confidence by talking with Bea and Sid Parnes about his creativity. His mentors really helped him to understand himself better. Does your school have a mentorship program, where students can work with adults, college students, high school students, or even grandparents on a special area of interest? If your school doesn't have a mentorship program, find out what it would take to start one.

Resources

When Chad scored very high on the Torrance Test of Creative Thinking, the testing center invited Chad to be part of their mentorship program. To find out more about the test and the program, write to:

Dr. Bonnie Cramond
The University of Georgia
325 Aderhold Hall
Athens, GA 30602

"Yes I Can!" is a program that recognizes students who have addressed or overcome some personal or educational hurdles—including kids like Chad, who is gifted *and* learning disabled. To find out more about it, write or call:

The Foundation for Exceptional Children
1920 Association Drive
Reston, VA 22091
(703) 620-1054

There are many books available on creativity and creative thinking. Look for these in your library, and ask your librarian for other recommendations:

Frederick by Leo Lionni (Knopf, 1990). This picture book for children of all ages tells how an unconventional mouse named Frederick brings color and joy into the drab winter surroundings he shares with his friends.

Oliver Dibbs and the Dinosaur Cause by Barbara A. Steiner (Four Winds Press, 1986). Ollie, a resourceful boy, leads a drive to have the Stegosaurus named the Colorado State Fossil. Based on a true story, this book demonstrates how creativity can affect events and governments.

Find out more about learning problems by reading these books:

Different Not Dumb by Margot Marek (Franklin Watts, 1985). Second grader Mike has a reading disability, but he finds both help and hope when he is placed in a special reading program. In fact, he even begins to outread some of his classmates!

The Survival Guide for Kids with LD (Learning Differences) by Gary Fisher, Ph.D., and Rhoda Cummings, Ed.D. (Free Spirit Publishing, 1990). Learn what it's like to grow up with LD, why kids with LD have trouble learning, and more.

Sixth Grade Can Really Kill You by Barthe DeClements (Viking Penguin, 1985). Helen Nichols has a learning disability and finally finds school success in a special education class that meets her academic and social needs.

II

OVERCOMING A VISUAL IMPAIRMENT:
The Story of Allyson Matt

Allyson calls her home town of Ft. Wayne, Indiana, a "pretty big city." The two-story house she shares with her parents and four-year-old sister, Emily, is in a quiet neighborhood. "My house is on a cul de sac," Allyson explains, "which is a street that dead ends, but instead

FAMILY AND BACKGROUND

of having to turn around in someone else's driveway, the street goes in a circle at the end and puts you back in the same direction you came."

Nine-year-old Allyson describes a cul de sac so perfectly that you can actually see it in your mind. But Allyson herself has never seen the street on which she plays, or the house in which she lives. "I don't think there are any interesting facts about me except for my being visually impaired, which is something I have to live with because I don't think it's going to change, at least right now it isn't," she says. She prefers the term "visually impaired" over "blind." She thinks it sounds better, and so do other people she knows who also have visual impairments.

An avid sports fan and participant, fourth grader Allyson has many interests and hobbies: riding her bike, swimming, playing kickball, collecting rocks, and playing with her friends. She also enjoys "listening to good books and records," and is just now learning to play the trumpet. Nothing seems to slow her down.

MAKING A
DIFFERENCE

Allyson is good at many things that some people might consider big accomplishments for anyone her age, especially someone with a disability. But she considers them pretty typical. "I really don't think I have done any project, activity, or event that is really special," Allyson reports. "Probably the reason people recognize me is because of the accomplishments I have made even though I'm visually impaired."

While Allyson insists that there is "nothing special" about her life, she does note that she has been able to achieve some goals that many people would never expect a child with a visual impairment to master. She is especially proud of these:

- She taught herself how to jump rope—single and double-dutch—and how to ride a bicycle without training wheels.

- She learned to ice skate and roller skate.

- At age four, she began to read and write in Braille. You may think that Braille is just 26 letters of the alphabet. Think again! "It has about 250 contractions, word signs, and short-form words," Allyson says. "For example, 'st' has its own sign, and by itself it means 'still.' Math also has its own signs and symbols, called Nemeth Code, so you don't get the numbers mixed up with the letters."

- She enrolled in a gifted program in first grade. According to her, this is "not a big deal. Just because I'm visually impaired doesn't mean I'm not smart."

Another accomplishment Allyson recognizes is her own "I-can-do-it" attitude. She doesn't just sit around feeling sorry for herself because she can't do everything sighted children can.

"Sometimes I feel bad about not being able to see movies and TV," she admits. "Really, I would like to see mostly everything. I used to feel bad when people were playing tag or hide-and-seek and I couldn't play. When I can't see where my friends are, I can't see where they are hiding."

Her advice for other kids who are visually impaired is simple: "Deal with what is wrong, and if it gets fixed, be happy, but if not, then just live with it. You may not be able to do some things, but you will be able to do other things that sighted kids can't do."

Even an attitude as positive as Allyson's can't make a disability go away. And yes, her visual impairment does prevent her from participating in some activities, which bothers Allyson and her parents.

LESSONS LEARNED

For example, when Allyson wanted to play soccer, her mother and father said no. They didn't think it was appropriate for someone who couldn't see the ball. So Allyson took up swimming instead. As a compromise to soccer, she plays kickball with her family.

In general, Allyson's parents have urged her to explore her interests. "They have encouraged me to try different things, like riding a bike, running, and climbing," Allyson says. "They want me to experience things sighted people can so I'll be outgoing and not as cautious."

In school, Allyson has a special teacher, Ms. Nighswander, who takes her reading and writing assignments and "translates" them into Braille. The only time a problem occurs is when her regular teachers forget to give the assignments to Ms. Nighswander, and Allyson has too much reading to do all at once.

In addition to helping Allyson with her school work, Ms. Nighswander has helped her to accept and live with her disability. "She has talked to me when I have had a hard time dealing with being visually impaired," Allyson reports. "She has told me that she understands that it hurts. She has told me I can do or be just about anything I want. I just have to figure out a way to adapt."

A continuing question for Allyson is whether or not she would be a better problem solver if she were sighted. "I have to rely on my hearing and memory more to figure out clues in the problems I hear, so I have to listen better," she explains. "Unlike other people, I can't draw a picture to help me out."

PERSONAL GOALS, GLOBAL CONCERNS

When Allyson considers her future, she thinks of several careers that interest her. For example, she might become a chiropractor, a professional who treats people's health problems by manipulating and massaging the back. "As long as someone tells me what the X-rays say, then I could adjust the person's back by feeling what's out of place," she says. Or she might choose to be a teacher for children who are gifted, or visually impaired—or both.

Pollution bothers Allyson, and she would like to make her world a cleaner and greener place. "I would like to have more trees, because people are cutting them down too fast and animals are losing their homes," she explains.

For the present, though, Allyson is happy with her life. There is only one thing she would like to change: She wishes that more girls her age lived in her neighborhood. This may happen sooner than she thinks; Allyson and her family are preparing to move to another state. Perhaps there she will have more neighborhood playmates. And maybe they can help her to realize one of her biggest dreams: to invent a way for people with visual impairments to play sports like soccer.

kidstories

"Sometimes I don't think it's fair that I can't see," Allyson says. "I know I can't play soccer and other sports, but I know I *can* play some sports. Sometimes I won't be able to do everything sighted kids can, but that's life. Because even though I am visually impaired, I know that there are a lot of things I can do."

Allyson Matt has learned to live with her disability. Thanks to her parents, her teachers, and her positive attitude toward life, she has also learned to excel.

Questions to Consider

1. When people—adults and children—meet a person with a physical disability, they often feel uncomfortable or unsure of what to say. Why do you think this is so? Are there any specific ways you can suggest that might help others to see people with disabilities as "real people," with emotions and intellects that are not hampered by their physical condition?

2. "Just because I'm visually impaired doesn't mean I'm not smart," Allyson observes. Why do some people continue to believe the stereotype that people who are "different" can't possibly be intelligent? What can you do to prove to people how silly and cruel these stereotypes can be? Is there anything you can start in your school to educate others about disabilities?

Resources

If you haven't yet read the story of Helen Keller, now is a good time to learn more about this remarkable woman. She overcame visual and hearing impairments, graduated from college with honors, became a writer and lecturer, and was awarded the Presidential Medal of Freedom. Many books have been written about Helen Keller; here are two suggestions:

For elementary students: *Helen Keller: A Light for the Blind* by Kathleen V. Kudlinski (Viking Kestrel, 1989).

For older readers: *Helen and Her Teacher: The Story of Helen Keller and Anne Sullivan Macy* by Joseph P. Lash (Delacorte Press, 1980).

If you like to read plays, get a copy of *The Miracle Worker* by William Gibson, a play based on Helen's early life. Or, if you'd rather see the movie of the play, there are two versions available: the first, made in 1962, stars Patty Duke, and a later one, made in 1979, stars Melissa Gilbert. Both are on video.

Read more about young people with physical impairments. Check your library for these and other books:

The Absolute, Ultimate End by Julia First (Franklin Watts, 1985). Maggie Thayer has a rewarding 8th-grade year when she becomes an advocate for a visually impaired girl she tutors.

Don't Feel Sorry for Paul by Bernard Wolf (J.B. Lippincott, 1974) chronicles two weeks in the life of a boy with deformed hands and feet.

Mom Can't See Me by Sally Hobart Alexander (Macmillan, 1990). Sally Hobart Alexander is a successful children's author who also happens to be blind. This is a true story about her, told from her nine-year-old-daughter's point of view.

Move Over, Wheelchairs Coming Through by Ron Roy (Clarion, 1985) includes the life stories of seven young people whose physical impairments require them to use wheelchairs.

To learn more about visual impairments, write or call:
American Council for the Blind
1010 Vermont Avenue, NW, Suite 1100
Washington, D.C. 20005
(800) 424-8666

For information about spoken books and books for the visually impaired, write or call:
Recording for the Blind, Inc.
20 Roszel Road
Princeton, NJ 08540
(609) 452-0606

National Library Services for the Blind
and Physically Handicapped
1291 Taylor Street, NW
Washington, D.C. 20452
(202) 707-5100

12

LIVING ON TOP OF THE WORLD:
The Story of Wayne E. Floyd

C olorado and Alaska have a lot in common: mountains to climb, snow to shovel, and lots of beautiful wide open spaces. Alaska, though, has so many wide open spaces, and so few people to fill them, that even Colorado's expansive wilderness areas look small in comparison to those found in our 49th state.

Wayne Floyd has experienced both of these worlds first-hand. He now attends the United States Air Force (USAF) Academy in Colorado Springs, Colorado, a city almost half as populous as all of Alaska. But his school years were spent in Skwentna, Alaska, a town he describes as "a rural, 'bush' community 70 miles northwest of Anchorage." Wayne lived there with his parents, Vernon and Kazuko, his brother, Arthur, their pet dog, Bubba, and the family cat, April.

Skwentna doesn't have a shopping mall, or even a convenience store. "There are no roads, electricity, water, or other common public services," Wayne says, "except a post office and a school." Only about 100-150 people live within a 30-mile radius. Wayne's school was a K-12 building with about 20 students in all. And it was not around the corner or a few blocks away. It was 17 miles from where Wayne and his family lived. He traveled to school by snowmobile or boat, depending on the season.

Currently in his freshman year at the Academy, Wayne enjoys fishing (salmon and trout), reading (especially science fiction), military aviation, and role-playing games like Dungeons and Dragons.

MAKING A
DIFFERENCE

Being selected to attend any United States military academy, like the USAF Academy or West Point, is quite an accomplishment. More than 60,000 students per year send for information about the USAF Academy. About 12,000 of these complete the demanding application process, which includes an interview, a writing sample, and an analysis of high school transcripts and extracurricular activities.

It also includes a physical fitness test, which, according to Wayne, "is *definitely not* like your typical gym class." It must be conducted at the nearest Air Force facility. And before their applications can even be processed, students must be nominated by a U.S. Senator or Representative. Out of 60,000 interested students, only 1,400 are chosen to enroll in each year's freshman class.

Wayne was able to successfully complete all of these application requirements, an achievement that makes him feel proud. What makes his achievement even more remarkable is the fact that he seldom even attended school—at least, not in the usual way. In fact, very little about Wayne's education was typical.

As he explains it, "From first through fifth grade, I was taught by my mother at home. My mom's not a teacher, but she has a degree in literature from a Japanese university. I attended a regular public school in Skwentna from grades six through eight, and for high school, I earned about two-thirds of my graduation credits through correspondence courses."

Wayne's unique approach to high school was sponsored and paid for by his school district. Since Wayne's school had so few students, it was impossible for it to offer certain math, English, and science courses Wayne needed. So he applied to a program made available by the University of Nebraska at Lincoln.

Here's how it worked. Wayne's professors in Nebraska sent him the books and materials he needed for a physics or trigonometry course. Then Wayne completed his assignments and sent them to the University. When Wayne felt ready to be tested, he informed the principal at his school. (Usually, there were four or five tests per course, plus a final exam.) He took the tests, his school sent them to the University of Nebraska, and his professors there graded them.

Occasionally, there were problems with this arrangement. Sometimes Wayne needed fast answers to questions; he couldn't wait several weeks to hear from his Nebraska professors. But it wasn't always easy to find someone nearby. "For example," Wayne recalls, "if I hit an area of study none of my teachers understood—say, in physics—my principal had to call other, larger school districts to find someone to answer my question."

Still, Wayne graduated with a 3.7 grade point average, good enough to earn him the honor of class valedictorian (in a class of four students). "It was a great and exhilarating experience to graduate as valedictorian," Wayne says. "High school was over and done with, and I was looking forward to the rest of my life, college especially."

What does he think of his small, out-of-the-way Alaskan "bush" school? "Skwentna School prepared me well for my life," he replies, "particularly in teaching me about how determination, perseverance, and dedication can help you get something done; and in teaching me that I had those qualities."

LESSONS LEARNED

Although Wayne took many of his high school subjects through independent study, he still had to report to school each day. This was complicated by the fact that there were no school buses, and the 17-mile trip was too far to walk. Plus there were other problems unique to Alaska.

"Every day," Wayne explains, "I would have to deal with various inclement situations. There were days when the snowmobile trails were covered with too much snow, or when moose became argumentative about who deserved to use the trails, showing their displeasure by charging me or my friends." And on days when he would rather have pulled the bed covers back over his head, Wayne still had to travel to school.

He recalls that "when I would wake up and find 18 inches of new snow on the trail, I knew it was going to take much longer and was going to be a hard trip. One way I kept myself motivated and eager was through some 'macho reasoning': 'If I don't go, I'll be a wimp.' Or I would think, 'Won't they be impressed if I show up at school, even with all this snow?' This, and my desire to learn, usually were enough to keep me going."

Throughout his years of going to school in Skwentna, Wayne had the constant help of his mother and father. "My parents not only gave me love and support all through the seven years I traveled to Skwentna School," he remembers, "but early in my life they instilled in me a love of learning. They were always encouraging me to read and to do well in school."

His mother, in addition to being his teacher for five years, always saw that Wayne had the resources he needed, like encyclopedias. Also, she made sure to keep in touch with Wayne's principal, informing him when Wayne needed special help or an added "boost."

"And my father always told me," Wayne says, "that he had spent 20 years on the wrong end of a shovel, in his job as a pipe layer. He's proud of his work—so am I—but he wanted me to do more; to develop my leadership abilities."

Very willing to heed his father's advice, Wayne plans a career in aviation, probably in the area of airborne radar operation. When he was younger, Wayne dreamed of becoming a pilot, "but when I got eyeglasses in fifth grade, I began to realize that I probably would never reach that goal. Although I was disappointed, I didn't let it bother me a lot, because there's still so much I can do related to aviation other than becoming a pilot."

Wayne's advice to others who need help in keeping their goals in focus? Simple and straightforward: "Stick with it. Finish what you are doing. No matter how bad the task may seem while you are doing it, you will be surprised—and probably pleased— with how it turns out."

"And one last thing," Wayne says, "about where my family chooses to live. Many times, when I explain to people the area of Alaska where I come from, they misunderstand me. When they hear 'rural,' they think of a farm in Iowa. Wrong in my case. Alaska's 'rural' is untamed wilderness with a house or two scattered about. Skwentna is wilderness, not rural. And it was a great place to grow up.

"When I reflect on my life in Skwentna, I have absolutely no regrets—I can talk with *anyone* and amaze them with my stories. I believe, too, that a lot of people, if they chose it, would love living the kind of life I've had."

Wayne has proved that geographic hardships and isolation do not result in a life, or an education, barren of meaning. True to the pioneering spirit fostered centuries ago by Alaska's early settlers, Wayne Floyd's spirit of determination continues to be his best teacher.

Questions to Consider

1. Write down a list of all of the free-time activities you participate in (or have access to) in your home town. Now make a list of activities you could take advantage of in Skwentna. Do some of the same items appear on both lists? Are there items on your home town list that you'd miss terribly if they weren't available? Are there items on the Skwentna list that you would dearly love to do? Compare the benefits of life in your town and life in Skwentna.

2. Most students get the opportunity, at some time, to work on an independent study project. In Wayne's case, the majority of his school life was spent on individual work. What are the benefits and drawbacks to the structure at Skwentna School? Would you like the chance to work independently more often than you do now? How much more independence would you like, and in what subjects? Are there any topics you would not want to study independently? Why not?

kidstories

Resources

Wayne's education was not a typical one. He had a "combination" education: some home schooling, some correspondence courses, some regular school.

Home schooling and correspondence courses are necessities for some students who live in rural areas and don't have access to the courses they want or need. But many students who don't live in rural areas are home schooled or take correspondence courses.

If you want to know more about home schooling, write to:
Growing Without Schooling
729 Boylston Street
Boston, MA 02116

Many books have been written about home schooling. Although these were written mainly for parents, you may find them interesting:

Homeschooling for Excellence by David and Micki Colfax (Warner Books, 1988). The kids in the Colfax family in Northern California have all been home schooled. Now they are going to Harvard.

Schooling at Home, edited by Anne Pederson and Peggy O'Mara (John Muir Publications, 1990). Information on full- and part-time schooling at home includes legal issues, different ways of educating at home, and stories about home schooling experiences.

Home Schools, An Alternative: You Do Have a Choice by Cheryl Border (Blue Bird Press, 1990). This book is a comprehensive guide for parents interested in educating their children at home.

Wayne earned most of his high school graduation credits through correspondence courses. If you would like to know more about correspondence courses, and maybe sign up for one or two, start by contacting the public university in your state. Wes Beach, an independent educational counselor in California, recommends Indiana University. You can call them toll-free at (800) 334-1011.

The Independent Study Catalog, edited by John H. Wells and Barbara C. Ready (Peterson's Guides, updated often), is a "big book" of high school and college correspondence courses. See if your library has a copy. Or, for more information, call the publisher toll-free at (800) EDU-DATA (that's 800-338-3282).

If, after reading Wayne's story, you'd like to learn more about Alaska, have a look at *Alaska* by Ann Heinrichs (Children's Press, 1991). You'll find lots of information about and pictures of this fascinating frontier state.

13

A REFUGEE FROM VIOLENCE:
The Story of Stephanie Auxila

I t's never easy, especially when you're a kid, to pick up and move to a new home. It's even harder when that new home is so far removed from your old one that you can't even call or visit your friends.

Imagine, then, how difficult it would be to move to a new country, whose customs and language are as foreign to you as yours appear to other people. That's what happened to Stephanie Auxila, a nine-year-old girl now living in Miami, Florida, who escaped from war-torn Haiti when she was only six years old.

But more about that later. Here's what Stephanie is doing now: "I live in a nice townhouse with my grandparents and my mother, but I'll soon move into a small apartment with just my mom. I am an only child, and my parents are divorced."

Stephanie attends a bilingual international school because her mother does not want her to forget French, her native language. When she has free time, Stephanie likes to play tennis, read books, and listen to music. Swimming, jogging, and jumping rope keep her physically fit, as does "trying to imitate my mother when she dances to Haitian music." Her grandfather is very special to her, and one of her favorite activities is "listening to Grandpa's stories."

MAKING A DIFFERENCE

Coming to America was not something that Stephanie and her family had ever planned to do. Then, in 1987, Stephanie's native country of Haiti experienced major political turmoil. The country's dictator, Jean-Claude Duvalier, left Haiti suddenly to avoid being captured—and almost certainly killed—by the people he had oppressed and tortured for so many years.

Shortly after Duvalier fled, elections were called. These were to be the first free elections in Haiti in decades, yet many people still loyal to Duvalier feared what the election results might be. On the morning of the elections, violence erupted throughout the country. Dozens of citizens waiting to vote were killed by soldiers who hoped for Duvalier's return.

Among those who were shot at, but who escaped with their lives, were Stephanie, her mom, and her grandfather, the Reverend Alain Rocourt, Chairman of Haiti's Methodist Church. Hundreds of submachine gun shots were fired into the house where Stephanie and her family resided, and hand grenades were tossed in, too. Miraculously, the entire family survived the attack by cowering on the floor of their house.

kidstories

A second machine gun attack occurred soon after the first, and Stephanie and her family feared that they would not survive much longer. The target of these attacks was Stephanie's grandfather, a leader of the Democratic Elections Committee.

What followed was a series of harrowing escapes from their home. One by one, Stephanie and her family were smuggled out of their house after nightfall. Then they were taken to Haiti's International Airport for passage out of the country.

Unaware of her family's escape plan, Stephanie just did as she was told by the strangers who brought her to the airport. As she remembers it, "I was the last person in my family to leave Haiti, and I was put on a plane with strangers. I didn't know where I was going, and I was afraid I was never going to see my mother again."

Finally arriving at the Miami Airport—afraid, alone, and able to speak only French and Creole—Stephanie was overwhelmed with joy to find her family awaiting her arrival. With the help of her grandfather's friends from the Methodist Church, Stephanie and her mother settled into a small, crowded, but safe apartment.

The next year, Stephanie's grandfather was given political asylum by the U.S. Department of Justice, which also allowed Stephanie and her mom to remain in America as political refugees. This meant that they would not have to return to Haiti until the trouble had subsided and life was safe once again. Most recently, all of Stephanie's family was granted permanent residency status in the United States. Now they can stay in America for as long as they wish.

W ith the horror of political repression behind them, Stephanie and her family began to get used to their new lives in Miami. There were, of course, many things to which Stephanie needed to adjust, the most obvious being the English language.

LESSONS
LEARNED

"I could not understand people, so I could not do what I was told," Stephanie recalls. "So I always went to the end of the line and watched what others did first, and then I imitated them. The one thing I could not change was the strange look on people's faces when they heard I was Haitian. Even now, they believe it's weird that I am Haitian, because I am not *really* black, like many people from my country are."

But Stephanie had help adjusting to America, and her neighbors and classmates learned to adjust to this girl who seemed so unlike them. "My family, my teachers, and my new friends encouraged me and helped me feel I was not different from other kids just because I was from Haiti," Stephanie remembers.

Today, more than three years since her arrival in Miami, Stephanie has mastered English, and a whole lot more. Now she realizes that she can both succeed—she made the honor roll in second grade—and fit in. Still, she wishes that people would respect one another for reasons that go beyond appearance. "People should not be judged because of their color or where they are from," she insists. "Even if someone looks ugly from the outside, they can be beautiful inside."

Stephanie knows that appearances can be deceiving. "Life may look simple, but it is not always so," she says.

PERSONAL GOALS, GLOBAL CONCERNS

Maybe it's due to the support she received in adjusting to life in America—or maybe it's for a far different reason—but Stephanie plans to become a psychologist someday. She wants "to help people who have problems they keep in their heads and that other people do not understand."

Stephanie's not sure if she wants to return to Haiti ("I do not remember much about it"), but she is sure that she wants a new, American-based family. "I would like for my mom to remarry," she says, "and give me a brother and a sister so I can experience life in a family of my own, with another father."

Speaking of family, Stephanie believes that we should learn to see our world's population as a single, very big one, and the place to start is the United States. "I would add classes that would tell students more about people in other countries and their lives," she explains. "Many Americans do not know what is happening in the world."

kidstories

Lastly, based on her experiences in Haiti, Stephanie thinks that our whole planet needs to refocus its efforts. "I would like for people to concentrate on cleaning the air and finding solutions to the hunger problem, instead of preparing for stupid wars," she says.

What advice would Stephanie give to others? "Don't get discouraged by something that seems difficult," she says. "Not everybody in this world is bad, and it is right to say out loud what you believe to people who want to influence you and make you become what you are not."

Questions to Consider

1. Stephanie remarks that Americans "do not know what is happening in the world." Do you believe she is right or wrong? What makes you think the way you do? From your own perspective, what do you believe Americans (or the people in your country) need to know about their global neighbors? What are some ways they might be educated about the world?

2. Learn something about Haiti's economy, political system, and past problems under Duvalier's regime. Compare lifestyles in Haiti with those in your own country. What are your conclusions about life in Haiti—today, and before Duvalier left and Stephanie Auxila came to the United States?

Resources

There are several organizations that help refugees from strife-torn countries, like Stephanie and her family. Other organizations provide humanitarian assistance to needy people within those countries. Here are some international and religious organizations you may want to learn more about:

Amnesty International
322 Eighth Avenue
New York, NY 10001
(212) 807-8400

Oxfam America
115 Broadway
Boston, MA 02116
(617) 728-2506

Save the Children
54 Wilton Road
Westport, CT 06880
(800) 243-5075

United Nations High Commissioner for Refugees
1718 Connecticut Avenue, NW
Washington, D.C. 20009
(202) 387-8546

The U.S. Committee for UNICEF
333 East 38th Street
New York, NY 10016
(212) 922-2508

kidstories

You learned that Stephanie is a refugee from Haiti. But do you know where Haiti is? If not, look it up in an atlas such as *Courage Children's Illustrated World Atlas* (Running Press, 1989). This book also gives you information about people from the different countries around the world.

Learn more about the world and its people. Visit your library and find these books and series:

Charlie Brown's Fourth Super Book of Questions and Answers about All Kinds of People and How They Live (Random House, 1979).

The Enchantment of the World Series (Children's Press, 1990). Each book in this series profiles a different country around the world. It includes more than 60 titles, from *Africa* to *Zimbabwe*.

The Families the World Over Series (Lerner, 1985-1990). Titles include *An Aboriginal Family, An Arab Family, A Family in France, A Family in Nigeria*, and so on. Also from the same publisher: The In America Series of 32 titles including *The Lebanese in America, The Puerto Ricans in America*, and so on.

So Far from the Bamboo Grove by Yoko Kawashima Watkins (Lothrop, Lee and Shepard, 1986). This book tells the true story of a Japanese girl who flees Korea at the end of World War II. Courage, determination, and the resilience of human beings emerge in the telling.

14

THE VOCATION OF A LIFETIME:
The Story of Maja Lynn North

When 18-year-old Maja North reflects on her recently completed high school career, she finds that many of her successes came as a result of being *away* from her alma mater, Grand Haven High School (GHHS). That's not to imply that she didn't enjoy GHHS. It just means that she found a perfect niche for herself at the Careerline Tech Center in a program for vocationally talented students.

First, though, some personal history. Maja lives outside of Grand Haven, Michigan, which she describes as "a tourist town with a beach, the 'World's Largest Musical Fountain,' a U.S. Coast Guard Station and, of course, tourists!" She loves her home town, and especially enjoys the farmhouse where she has lived since she was five years old. "It's in the woods," she says, "away from the city lights, with crickets who sing you to sleep every night."

Maja lives with her father and stepmother. Her siblings—two stepsisters and one stepbrother—are all married. Other siblings live with Maja's birth mother, Sandi, in California. Although Maja doesn't see them too often, she managed a visit recently. "It was a special time for all of us," Maja says. "We all needed it."

Maja enjoys running, biking, and swimming, and plans to enter several triathlons—athletic contests that involve these three sports—over the next ten years. Photography ranks as one of her interests, as does going to church. "I know that sounds strange," she admits, "but my church has that 'life' in it that I've never found anywhere else."

MAKING A DIFFERENCE

At Grand Haven High School, Maja was a top student, earning high honors for her academic performance, including a straight-A average in her senior year. But she is proudest of her participation in the RISE program at a local vocational high school.

RISE gives students the chance to explore their talents in any of 31 vocational areas, ranging from food services to industrial and mechanical arts, business management, and graphic arts (Maja's specialty). Students in RISE work with teachers and community based mentors who are experts in their fields.

For Maja, RISE was an opportunity to develop her artistic abilities, and it was a chance to expand her options beyond the limits of the regular classroom. She did extremely well.

"In my first year in RISE, as a junior, I won 9 of the 11 contests I entered," she says. "In a statewide portfolio contest, I

kidstories

placed second against 115 other vocational students. This shocked me!"

As a result of her successes in art, Maja was selected to attend a summer institute in photojournalism at Eastern Michigan University. There she was able to work with her peers and with talented artists. To Maja, the institute was "one of the most important events of my life, for personal reasons; I still keep in touch with some of the many friends I made there."

Recently Maja's high school principal nominated her for a statewide award for graduating seniors. Following a long and demanding selection process, Maja was named one of Michigan's Top 18 High School Graduates by the *Detroit News*. She was one of only two students selected for their vocational/technical achievements.

So far, everything in Maja's life sounds rosy and upbeat. And much of it has been. But Maja has also faced many obstacles on the way to achieving her goals, including growing up as a child in an alcoholic home, undergoing seven major surgeries, and surviving a car accident.

Although each of these has taken an emotional toll, Maja's personal strength—and her strong faith—have helped her through the roughest times. One of her most important influences is the Reverend Duane Vanderklok, her pastor at Resurrection Life Church. "I am thankful that I have a Godly, young, wise, knowledgeable, and awesome pastor!" she says.

M aja's surgeries took place between eighth and tenth grades, and all were operations on her feet. "I tried my best in sports," she remembers, "but when you have a cast, it's hard to run and swim." Then, in 1988, her car was hit by someone who ran a stop sign at 60 miles per hour.

LESSONS LEARNED

Her passenger died of injuries, and Maja herself sustained multiple injuries including a broken neck, fractured skull, ruptured spleen, and closed head injuries. She went in and out of comas, and doctors told her parents that she would need extensive rehabilitation—if she lived. However, Maja refused to die. "To make a long story short," she says, "through the prayers of my friends, I am completely healed and am doing better than ever before."

As she considers the crises and triumphs of her life, Maja is convinced that she has the inner strength to approach any obstacle she might meet in the future. "I feel that I am a changed person after all this has happened," she reflects. "My confidence and self-esteem have been built up. I know what my future direction and goals are now. I couldn't ask for anything more."

PERSONAL GOALS, GLOBAL CONCERNS

Currently enrolled at Kendall College of Art and Design, Maja plans to attend the Art Center College of Design in Pasadena, California. She would like to earn her Bachelor's degree and maybe a Master's degree in the advertising design field.

Some people have advised her to skip college and accept one of the many jobs she has already been offered, but she's determined to go to college first. Later, she hopes to become an art director.

When it comes to her hopes for the world, Maja wishes that more people would look to faith for guidance and what she calls "knowing." By this, she means "to have the knowledge of, to understand completely, to investigate the truth, and then to put that knowledge to work." At that point, she believes, "knowledge becomes wisdom."

To improve school, Maja would pay teachers higher salaries, for starters. She would also like to see "goal setting, zeal for life, and ambition instilled in the classes, the students, and the teachers."

What advice would she give to other students her age? Asked this question, Maja provides a recipe that could guide many adults: "Commit yourself to excellence in your physical self, your attitude toward people and life, and your spirituality. Write your goals down so you can see them all the time and not forget about them. It helps you to push forward and accomplish things that you've always wanted to do. As Dr. Abraham Maslow, a psychologist, once wrote, 'One can choose to go back toward safety or forward, toward growth. Growth must be chosen again and again; fear must be overcome again and again.' Reach forward is my advice."

Success is never really achieved until one believes in the worth of one's efforts. Thanks to so many opportunities to grow and learn, and due to the support of educators, friends, family, and faith, Maja North has succeeded.

Questions to Consider

1. Maja reports that although she has been tempted by several job offers, she plans to go to college first. But several people (including some artists) have encouraged her to take a job instead. If you were Maja, and good job offers came your way, what factors would you use to determine whether you would accept a job or pursue a college education?

2. Often, schools don't seem to care as much about vocational talents as academic ones. Does your own school provide programs and alternatives for students who are especially talented in the arts, electronics, auto mechanics, or other vocational areas? If few or no options exist, ask "the people in charge" why these strengths are not addressed.

Resources

Participation in the RISE program changed Maja's life and set her on a clear career path. To find out more about this program, write to:

> **Careerline Tech Center**
> **Project Coordinator**
> **13663 Port Sheldon Road**
> **Holland, MI 49424**

Students in RISE work with community-based mentors—adult experts in specific fields. In Minnesota, a program called Mentor Connection gives high school students in the Minneapolis-St. Paul area a chance at mentorships. Students in Mentor Connection have explored careers in creative writing, music, computer science, health science, marketing, engineering, design, law, artificial intelligence, psychology, journalism, public relations, medicine, architecture, business, veterinary medicine, wildlife management, photography, aeronautical engineering, biochemistry, jazz composition, graphic arts, and many more. To find out more about Mentor Connection, write or call:

> **Jill Reilly**
> **Mentor Connection**
> **Intermediate District 917**
> **1300 E. 145th Street**
> **Rosemount, MN 55068**
> **(612) 423-8479**

To find out how your school can set up mentorships, get a free copy of *One on One: A Guide for Establishing Mentorship Programs.* Write to:

> **U.S. Department of Education**
> **400 Maryland Avenue, SW**
> **Washington, D.C. 20202-4110**

Are you an artist like Maja? Or do your talents run more to photography? Would you like to be able to sell your work? Check your library for copies of *Artist's Market* and *Photographer's Market* (both from Writer's Digest Books, updated annually). For more information, write to:

> **Writer's Digest Books**
> **1507 Dana Avenue**
> **Cincinnati, OH 45207**

HELP IS
ON THE WAY

There are a lot of words in our language that describe good deeds and kind acts. *Philanthropy* is what happens when wealthy people give money to good causes or non-profit organizations. *Charity* is a more personal form of philanthropy, something done by anyone who writes out a check to Greenpeace or drops a dollar in the Salvation Army's red kettle during the rush of holiday shopping. People of all kinds give *contributions* to worthy causes, or make *donations* to their local food bank or Goodwill store.

What do all of these actions have in common? Much more than money. Each is inspired by an ideal: "My help can make a difference."

In this section, you will read about young people who reached out when they saw that something wasn't right, something wasn't done, or someone was in pain. Their personal actions seldom involved money, yet the collective contributions they have made for our world are worth their weight in gold. Not content to wait until they were old enough to write checks or rich enough to donate millions, these kids took it upon themselves to make a difference now—today.

Presenting the greatest gift of all—compassion for other human beings—each person in the stories that follow realized truths that some other people seek for a lifetime: that one person *can* make a difference; that each person's actions do count; and that life satisfaction can be gauged by a unit of measure called "love."

People often complain that the TV news is filled with sad and negative stories—the "dirty laundry" of our neighbors on this planet. Newspapers, too, seem to focus most on crimes, disasters, and other grim events. There is no denying that bad things happen, and we all have a right to know about them. But just as a diet of junk food may fill your stomach yet leave you nutritionally empty, a steady diet of personal pain and tragedy will leave you with a weakened spirit.

Here, as a healthy alternative, are some reasons to celebrate. These stories will provide balance and sustenance to your mind and your emotions. Help is on the way, and it comes in the form of young people who took the time to care.

15

MAKING SOCIAL STUDIES COME TO LIFE:
Ellsworth Middle School Grade 7-3 Geography Class

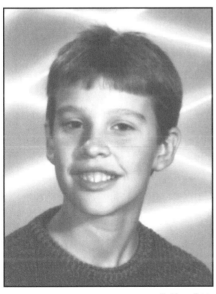

D. Marc Fetty

Each of the other biographies in *Kidstories* focuses on an individual—someone with a home and a family. This one is about the 25 individuals in Mrs. Diana Stender's 7-3 Geography Class. Their "home" is Ellsworth Middle School in Middlebourne, West Virginia. And they share many of the same qualities often found in families: love, togetherness, respect, and a common goal of helping other people.

Middlebourne is a small, rural town of about 900 people. It doesn't have a Dairy Queen or a stoplight, but there are many advantages to living here. According to eighth grader D. Marc Fetty, "Middlebourne has a very minor drug problem and a high percentage of students being able to participate in extracurricular activities." It is a town of "traditional values like a strong belief in God, pride in our country, and respect for others."

MAKiNG A DiFFERENCE

This respect for others shows in a project Mrs. Stender does every year with her seventh graders. Each fall, as the school year begins, Mrs. Stender's students look around their community and their world for problems that need solving. Students tackle projects individually, in pairs, and sometimes as an entire class. They submit their projects to the West Virginia Social Studies Fair, an annual competition involving dozens of school districts within the state.

At the Fair, the projects are separated into divisions (elementary, middle school, and high school) and judged. The judges look for things like thoroughness and how much a project helped others.

A couple of years ago, the 7-3 Geography Class combined several projects under the title of "Small But Mighty: We Can Make Things Happen." Marc Fetty and Susie Mercer were the spokespersons for the project. According to them, "Small But Mighty" was quite diverse.

"We collected toys and baby supplies for an orphanage in Ecuador," they explain. "We wrote letters to State officials and helped obtain funding for a local senior citizens center. We studied the effects of what might happen if our school consolidated with other schools, and our county superintendent of schools took our results with her when she attended state meetings to get funds for consolidation.

"We each 'adopted' a grandparent and sent them cards, called them on the phone, and did small helping jobs for them. We collected scrap metal and gave the proceeds from its sale—

kidstories

several hundred dollars—to a boy named Johnny Hollingshead, in Wheeling, West Virginia, who has leukemia. We each donated fifty cents to buy Johnny a sweatshirt to remember us by. We planted flowers at our school. Our class sponsored a Patriotic Essay Contest."

It's hard to believe that one class did all that, but it's true. The judges at the Social Studies Fair were impressed: They gave Ellsworth's 7-3 Geography Class several awards, including First Prize for the entire project. They also gave the class the Grand Prize for presenting their project in the most entertaining way.

In addition to awarding first prize to the class, the contest judges presented two students, Stephanie Patterson and Missy Goots, with the Third Place prize in the pairs competition for their project on school consolidation. Because of the work done by Stephanie and Missy, a new $15 million middle school/high school will be built to serve the students of Tyler County, where Middlebourne is located.

Stephanie was one of the students who won individual awards for particular projects. Yet she insists that "Small But Mighty" benefited the entire class. "More important than all the awards was what we accomplished," she says. "We learned we can really make a difference, and even though we were only 13 years old, we helped our school, our community, and our superintendent. And we gained confidence in ourselves."

N aturally the 7-3 students and their teachers at Ellsworth School are proud of their *individual* accomplishments. But what's most noticeable is their sense of *collective* pride. As Marc Fetty points out, "I want everyone to understand that this project was a *class* project. We all worked together."

LESSONS LEARNED

Mrs. Stender, their teacher, was a catalyst in helping her students realize their goals. "She gave the most important things anyone could give—her time and a lot of effort," Marc says. "She scheduled field trips, pointed us in the right directions for our research, and helped us learn how important each of our project ideas was."

With help from one another, the students also learned a powerful lesson. As Marc puts it, "If you don't dream the highest dream and shoot for the goal, then you'll never make it."

Speaking of "making it," it's interesting to see how "Small But Mighty" changed the way the students felt about themselves and their future. At the beginning of the project, Mrs. Stender asked her students to review their personal goals for life after high school graduation. She found that most students had no idea about their possible careers—in fact, some students had doubts that they would even complete high school.

Then came "Small But Mighty." Afterward, all seventh grade students could name at least one career they might consider—from lawyer to veterinarian, Air Force officer, or professional baseball player. (As one student observed, "I want to set an example, like Roberto Clemente did.") Also, every student had plans to complete high school. There was no more talk of dropping out.

PERSONAL GOALS, GLOBAL CONCERNS

With projects that ranged from local issues to global concerns—from "adopt-a-grandparent" to helping children in Ecuador—the 7-3 Geography students saw the need to improve our planet through communication.

What were some of their wishes? "To see all Vietnam War POW's returned home, to have all countries enjoy the freedom found in America, and to wipe out racism, prejudice, war, drug and alcohol abuse, and satanism." And how could these things happen? "Our world could be a much improved place to live if we could work together and improve these things," the students say. From a little corner of America come fine ideas for global change.

Stephanie Patterson, speaking for herself and her classmates, advises students to remember that they *can* make a difference in the lives of others. "If there is any project at all in your school or community," she says, "or if you feel there needs to be one, don't be afraid to show you're interested. One small candle can light the way for you to see, and even though you are only one, you can touch the lives of many.

kidstories

"Take charge of your life, have confidence, and you can make a difference. Even if you don't win 'the prize,' you are a winner knowing that you did your best."

Questions to Consider

1. Find Middlebourne, West Virginia, on a U.S. map (remember...7-3 was a geography class!). Compare its locale and surroundings to where you live. How do you think your life would be different if you lived in Middlebourne? How would it be the same? On a scale of 1 to 10 (1 = blah, 10 = great), rate your interest in living in a town like Middlebourne. Explain your answer.

2. Think about all of the projects the 7-3 kids did. In your opinion, which one was the most important? Discuss your response with a friend or classmate who has a different "favorite project." Explain to each other why you chose the project you did.

Resources

Perhaps you've collected money for UNICEF at Halloween, or sent their cards at Christmas. UNICEF develops and implements social service, health, nutrition, and educational programs that help underprivileged children around the world. To find out what you can do, write or call:

UNICEF
Three United Nations Plaza
New York, NY 10017
(212) 326-7000

Save the Children is another organization that assists children, families, and communities in the U.S. and abroad. To learn more about it, write or call:

Save the Children
54 Wilton Road
Westport, CT 06880
(800) 243-5075

Does your state have a Social Studies Fair, like the one in West Virginia? Find out by asking your social studies teacher. If your teacher doesn't know, try contacting your State Department of Education. Ask to speak to the Social Studies Coordinator. If your state doesn't have a Social Studies Fair, maybe your school could sponsor one. Your social studies teacher can find out more about the West Virginia fair by writing or calling:

Dr. Barbara Jones
West Virginia Department of Education
Capitol Complex
Building 6, Room 330
Charleston, WV 25305
(304) 348-7805

16

SPEAKING OUT AGAINST CANCER:
The Story of Sarah Elisabeth Plunkett

At 14, Sarah Elisabeth Plunkett is the youngest of five children, and the only girl in her family. Her brothers are all in their 20's. One is a lawyer, another is in law school, one is a lieutenant in the Navy, and the other is a college senior. This leaves Sarah at home

FAMILY AND BACKGROUND

alone with her parents, her golden retriever, Caramel, and her two Siamese cats, Peanuts and Popcorn.

A native Texan, born and raised in the suburb of Plano, north of Dallas, Sarah is in the ninth grade at Vines High School. She describes herself as an avid "reader, listener, and watcher."

Currently she's into Tom Clancy novels, classic rock music (the Beatles, Elvis, the Stones, the Platters), and all kinds of movies. "I've seen some movies so many times I can recite them, even in my sleep," she says. She's also interested in speech and drama, and especially enjoys acting because "it lets me feel free and uninhibited."

MAKING A
DIFFERENCE

Like most adults, Sarah hates public speaking. There's nothing worse than getting up in front of a crowd of strangers, saying "Good evening ladies and gentlemen," and having to follow these words with a speech. Yet Sarah does this on a regular basis, and she's been doing it since she was 12 years old.

Sarah is a spokesperson for the Susan G. Komen Foundation, a Dallas-based group that works to advance public education, research, and testing of breast cancer. How did she start? "My class was assigned a History Fair project about an individual of our choice," she explains. "The national topic was, 'Does the individual make history, or does history make the individual?' I picked Nancy Brinker, the founder of the Komen Foundation."

As part of her project, Sarah spoke with Ms. Brinker, who was so impressed that she asked Sarah to become involved in the Foundation's nationwide campaign to educate people about breast cancer. And that meant public speaking.

"I speak in front of large groups of people—usually, potential corporate donors—on the ups and downs of cancer and chemotherapy," Sarah says. "I talk about how unfair this disease is, and that it is a destroyer of dreams. My one big problem is that I really get nervous before speaking. I try to tell myself that what I'm doing is really important, which usually helps."

Nancy Brinker started the Komen Foundation in 1982 after her sister, Susan G. Komen, died of breast cancer in 1980. With

Sarah's help, and the support of people like Marilyn Quayle, Barbara Bush, Betty Ford, and Jill Eikenberry, the Foundation has raised more than $7 million.

How did Sarah get interested in breast cancer in the first place? The answer to that question is found painfully close to home.

Sarah's mother, Kris, was diagnosed as having breast cancer in 1985. Kris had surgery and extensive chemotherapy, but the cancer kept spreading. In 1988 it entered her skull, breast bone, ribs, spine, and pelvic area.

"Mothers always dream of their children's first steps, first words, Little League games, ballet classes, proms, college, weddings, and grandkids," Sarah says. "But breast cancer can prevent one out of nine women from ever seeing those things.

"My mother might not even be around to see my high school graduation. Cancer is killing her, one step at a time. The reason I speak for the Foundation is because I feel it is my personal contribution in the war against breast cancer."

Even though she knows that her contribution is very important, Sarah still gets nervous before having to make a speech. "I have two problems that I can't do anything about," she explains. "One is that I always cry uncontrollably when I speak. The other is that when I speak, I am reminded of the fact that my mother is dying of cancer. But maybe I'm preventing some other kid's mom from dying, which makes me feel a little better."

Throughout her personal ordeal, Sarah has learned a lot about herself, about life, and about what it takes to make it—guts. She has also learned a lot about breast cancer, more than she thought she would ever need to know. And although she admits that she's still confused about cancer, and especially about why her mother had to get it, she knows that her goals are vital.

LESSONS LEARNED

"What I try to accomplish is very important—informing women about the need for mammography and self-examination," she asserts. "Maybe what's happened to my family won't happen to anyone else's."

kidstories

Sarah is continuing her crusade even beyond the Komen Foundation, as she has appeared with her mom three times on a nationally-syndicated TV show. She has also begun a project in her school to help teachers become more aware of how to work with students whose family members have cancer.

She has a lot of support from her family. "My brothers call me whenever I speak, and I call them whenever I need to. My mom tells me to go out and do it, and that she is very proud of me." Her friends help, too. "Karen and Alyssa are there for me whenever I need a shoulder to cry on. And Belinda, whose mom also has breast cancer, was a big support—she helped me to accept what was happening."

PERSONAL GOALS, GLOBAL CONCERNS

Sarah's other interests go in many and varied directions. She hopes to attend the University of Notre Dame and study either law or medicine. She likes law because two of her older brothers are in this field, and because "it's a logical profession, and I'm very into logic." She thinks about acting, although she's not sure if she'd want to make her living that way. Still, she admits that Hollywood or Broadway would be wonderful.

She describes her classes in school as "okay," but she'd like to change some of the other students' attitudes. "I wish they'd wake up and smell the coffee," she says. "They come to school only for the social aspect. Don't get me wrong—it's great to see your friends and all—but get a life! What you do now can and will affect the rest of your life. And I'm not a geeky bookworm. I just think that education is a privilege we shouldn't abuse."

Sarah's goals for a better world include more awareness about cancer, and a bond of international unity to promote world peace. Her brother in the Navy is stationed in Panama, so she is personally concerned about international relations.

For now, the Komen Foundation takes up most of her out-of-school energy and time. "For all my life," Sarah says, "I have watched my mother make homecoming, prom, or wedding dresses for other people. Maybe I'm selfish, but I want my mother to be around to make my dresses, too. Perhaps I can't

kidstories

have that, but maybe someone else's mom will be there to take prom pictures because they got that mammogram or practiced self-examination. I hope so."

Questions to Consider

1. Up until the time when Sarah met Nancy Brinker, the founder of the Komen Foundation, she dealt with the issue of breast cancer at home or with her friend, Belinda. How did Nancy Brinker change Sarah's life? What did she instill in Sarah that Sarah may not have had before they met? Is there anyone in your life (besides a relative, teacher, or family friend) who has changed your outlook on life or your approach to life because of a common bond or concern? Describe this person.

2. If you were Kris Plunkett, Sarah's mom, would you have encouraged her to pursue her work with the Komen Foundation? Remember how nervous Sarah always feels before public speaking (she even cries). Would it be better for her *not* to speak in public? Explain the reasons behind your answers.

Resources

Sarah is a spokesperson for the Susan G. Komen Foundation. To find out more about this organization, write or call:

> **Susan G. Komen Foundation**
> **6820(b) Freeway, Suite 130**
> **Dallas, TX 75240**
> **(800) I'M-AWARE (that's 800-462-9273)**

To find out about other cancer awareness and education groups in your area, write or call:

The American Cancer Society
1599 Clifton Road, NE
Atlanta, GA 30329
(800) 686-4357

Read about other young people who are coping with ill or aging family members. Check your library for these books, and ask your librarian for more recommendations:

Five Summers by JoAnn Bren Guernsey (Clarion, 1983). Mandy relives five summers of her life, which included dealing with her mother's battle with cancer. Over the years, Mandy learns many things about herself, her strengths, and the people around her.

Mollie Make-Believe by Alice Back (Harper & Row, 1974). Mollie's sixteenth summer is full of changes, including the illness and impending death of the grandmother she has always confided in.

Rabbit Ears: A Sports Novel by Robert Montgomery (New American Library, 1985). This first-person baseball novel revolves around Jason, a high school athlete, and his father, who contracted cancer from exposure to Agent Orange in Vietnam. Together, Jason and his family integrate their lives with that of their ill father in a positive, loving way.

The Ups and Downs of Jorie Jenkins by Betty Bates (Holiday House, 1978). Jorie's father, a doctor, is called to the hospital to treat a patient, then becomes a patient himself when he suffers a heart attack. This event drastically changes the lives of Jorie, a junior high school student, and her family.

17

GRACE UNDER PRESSURE, AND UNDER WATER:

The Story of Matt Heller

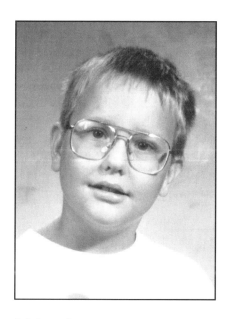

Matt is an eight-year-old fifth grader at

FAMILY AND BACKGROUND

Crestwood Elementary School in North Little Rock, Arkansas. He skipped first and third grades, so he's younger than most of his classmates. "Sometimes it's been hard being the youngest and smallest," Matt admits, "but I don't let it bother me."

Matt lives with his parents and his six-year-old brother, Sean. His many interests include all sports, especially soccer and swimming. Last year, Matt's team went to the state tournament in soccer. Matt also participated in the "Meet of Champs" swimming competition, where he placed fifth overall in the whole district and helped his relay team to a third-place finish.

In addition to sports, Matt enjoys math, geography, and English, although he does wish that some of his schoolwork was a bit more challenging. "I wish it was easier for someone who is good in a subject to move ahead faster," Matt says. He spends the rest of his free time in Boy Scouts and studying oceanography. He is particularly interested in learning about sharks because he thinks "they have a bad reputation."

When asked to sum up his life, Matt concludes that it's "pretty neat."

MAKING A DIFFERENCE

What is Matt most proud of in his life? You might think that the answer would come from among his many academic successes. In fact, the accomplishments he recalls most vividly have to do with two events not related to his classroom performance. "The first was a good one and the second was scary, but it turned out fine," he says.

His first memorable achievement was at the "Meet of Champs" swimming competition. Although both Matt and his team won medals, Matt never dreamed that this could happen.

"This was my first year on the swim team," he reports. "In the beginning, I was not very good—pretty bad, in fact! But I decided I wanted to push myself to do better."

Since the butterfly was his best stroke, Matt really worked hard on it. And with help from one of his relatives, he perfected his stroke to the point that he was able to compete successfully at swim meets.

The relative Matt credits for his progress is his Aunt Mary. "She really helped me in swimming. She is mentally retarded— she has Down's Syndrome—and is one of my best friends. She told me I could do it if I tried and worked hard. She showed me

kidstories

all the medals she had won at the International Special Olympics. I wanted her to be proud of me, so I worked really hard for her."

Some people might be surprised that a mentally disabled person could be a source of inspiration for a young athlete like Matt. But Aunt Mary's own personal achievements in the Special Olympics—a series of athletic events for disabled people modeled after the Olympics that you usually see on TV—and her encouragement to push himself beyond where he thought he could go, caused Matt to see her as a hero.

"My aunt told me I had to always try harder," Matt says. "She told me I had to improve my attitude." He did, and the results were amazing.

The second event that Matt recalls (the scary one) involved his younger brother, Sean. One day, while the two boys were walking home from school, Sean was hit by a car near their home. Since their parents were both at work, it was Matt who had to take charge of the emergency.

"I ran to a neighbor's house and got the adults to come," he says. "I ran back to the accident and helped get Sean out from under the car. I stayed with him and waited for the ambulance. The police came and questioned me. They were able to tell how fast the car was going by my answers and the skid marks.

"My parents were sent to the wrong hospital, so for a long time I was the only one with Sean. The doctors would tell me what they wanted Sean to do, and I would hold his hand and explain it to him. He had a neck brace on—they were afraid his back was broken—and his leg hurt a lot."

It turned out that Sean's leg was broken, but his back was okay. After a week in the hospital and eight weeks in a cast, Sean was as good as new. So was Matt.

"Sean was pretty scared," he remembers. "I was, too, but I didn't let him know. It was a pretty scary time, but I was glad I was there to help him. I was afraid my parents would blame me for the accident, but they didn't. They're pretty cool."

As Matt reflects on these two very different incidents from his life, he takes great pride in the way his efforts were rewarded. "I was proud of my swimming," he says. "I had reached a goal, and next summer I am going to try even harder. My soccer has gotten better, too!

"Sean's accident showed me that I could do pretty good in an emergency. I couldn't make him better, so I had to help in other ways. I wouldn't want to have to do it too often, though!"

With these accomplishments behind him, Matt is convinced that "you can do anything if you put your mind to it." In both his swimming successes and his take-charge attitude with Sean's accident, Matt found that staying calm was a prerequisite to doing a good job.

The ability to perform and excel under stressful conditions is the mark of a true winner, with true spirit. This is something Matt Heller knows personally, thanks to his own hard work and his inspiring coach, Aunt Mary.

As Matt continues to grow, he finds that he wants to learn from everyone around him, including his North Little Rock neighbors. "Most of my neighbors are old and don't come out much," he says. "I'd like to visit them and learn about them." This wish parallels Matt's desire to learn about different cultures and languages. He wishes there were more countries in the world.

At the age of eight, Matt Heller has learned a lesson that many adults still haven't mastered: It's possible to learn from anyone, at any time, if you give them and yourself a chance.

Questions to Consider

1. Matt's Aunt Mary is one of his "best friends" and inspirations, yet many people still believe that disabled persons can't teach anyone anything. What other examples can you find—in your own life, among your family and friends and neighbors, in literature or movies—that give further evidence that disabled people have special gifts or talents to share with others? Describe and discuss these examples.

2. Because Matt skipped two grades, he is the youngest and smallest in his fifth-grade class. If you had the choice, would you like to be placed in a grade level with older kids? What would be the drawbacks? What would be the benefits? If you have skipped one or more grades, how do you feel about this? If you haven't skipped grades, but a friend or sibling has, find out his or her feelings and opinions about grade skipping.

Resources

Matt's Aunt Mary won several medals by competing in the Special Olympics. Special Olympics International offers a worldwide program of training and competition in 22 sports for mentally disabled citizens ages 8 and up. You may want to get involved with this organization; perhaps you could help to train someone, or attend Special Olympics competitions in your area and cheer for the athletes. For more information, write or call:

> **Special Olympics International**
> **1350 New York Avenue, NW**
> **Suite 500**
> **Washington, D.C. 20005**
> **(202) 628-3630**

Can you imagine what it would be like to have a disabled family member? Most of us can't, unless we have actually experienced it. But you can read books about kids who have. Check your library for these, and ask your librarian for more ideas:

Half the Battle by Lynn Hall (Scribners, 1982). This book tells how two brothers deal with feelings of dependence and resentment caused by an older brother's blindness.

Making Room for Uncle Joe by Ada Bassett Litchfield (Whitman, 1984). When Dan's Uncle Joe comes to live with Dan's family, everyone is worried at first; Uncle Joe has Down's Syndrome. But apprehension turns to acceptance when family members see Uncle Joe as a loving and capable human being.

Straight from the Siblings by Gloria Murray and Gerald G. Jampolsky (Celestial Arts, 1982). This book describes the emotional and physical experiences of kids whose siblings have life-threatening illnesses.

LESSONS FROM THE EMERALD CITY

In *The Wizard of Oz*, each of the main characters is in search of something—a heart, a way home, a brain, and courage ("the noyve"). As the story unfolds, it becomes clear that each character already possesses whatever quality he or she desires.

The 1970's rock group, America, said it well in their song "Tin Man": "Oz never did give nothing to the Tin Man that he didn't already have." Which (except for the double negative) is an accurate statement that applies to most of us. Our whole potential lies within us at all times.

"People are like tea bags," novelist Rita Mae Brown observes. "You never know how strong they'll be until they're in hot water." The young people whose lives are highlighted in this section prove the truth of this statement. When confronted with situations that chafed against their moral or ethical principles, they had to decide which road to take—the easy trail of giving in and going along with the crowd, or the tougher path of sticking up for themselves and their convictions.

As you will read, sometimes the most difficult part of the journey came in choosing which road to take. At other times, the choice was easy but the consequences were hard. In all cases, these young people came up against practices, beliefs, or lifestyles that made them want to stand up and be counted as the thinking, feeling individuals they are.

Developing a philosophy of life, and then living according to this philosophy, is a journey that never ends. Like the yellow brick road to Oz, it contains many unmarked paths and hidden dangers. Still, as these biographies show, the exploration is worth the effort.

18

RUNNING FOR GLORY:
The Story of Nnenna Lynch

T he "Big Apple"— New York City— is Nnenna Lynch's home town. Although she now lives and goes to school in Pennsylvania, she is proud of her big-city background because "it has exposed me to so much and has led to my tolerance of people from all walks of life."

It's ironic that when

FAMILY AND BACKGROUND

Nnenna lived in New York, a city of seven million people, she attended the same school from kindergarten through high school. Hunter College Elementary and High School houses all students on the same campus. This means that Nnenna has known some of her friends and teachers since she was five years old.

As a 19-year-old college sophomore at Villanova University in Pennsylvania, Nnenna reflects on her years at Hunter. "I've known my best friend, Kysha, since nursery school," she says. "Both of our parents brought us into school a day early by accident, so we spent the day helping our teachers set up; Kysha and I have been friends ever since. Since she attends the University of Pennsylvania, only 20 minutes away, I still see her and speak to her often."

Nnenna, whose name comes from the African Igbo tribe and means "special woman," grew up with her mother and older sister, Shola. Her parents are divorced, but Nnenna often saw her father on weekends and vacations. Nnenna calls her sister a "me-do" kid—a "super-achiever who set a great example and set a high standard, which led me to my achievements." She also credits her mother with doing a great job of child-rearing, and says that "the older I get, the more I'm realizing how difficult a job that is."

Among Nnenna's hobbies are all sports, particularly biking and swimming. She plans to enter biathlons and triathlons in the future. She also has a fondness for "good conversation with intelligent and social people," all music "besides hard rock and elevator music," reading, dancing, the theater (stage, not movies), and good food.

MAKING A
DIFFERENCE

People who know Nnenna can think of numerous reasons why she should be proud of herself. They can point to her 3.87 grade point average during her freshman year at Villanova; they can cite the articles about Nnenna that have appeared frequently in *The New York Times* and other newspapers, reporting her accomplishments in cross-country track. They can even show you a copy of the December 1989 issue of *Vogue* magazine; Nnenna models on pages 126, 178, and 179.

Yet when Nnenna chooses to talk about something special in her life, she usually picks her accomplishments in track.

"I have been running with a club team since I was 10," she says. "I have won a number of state and national titles, as well as having broken state and national records." Her 1989 1,500-meter time of 4:29 is a United States record. In 1990, Nnenna helped Villanova win its second straight NCAA cross-country championship.

Nnenna's interest in athletics stems from Shola's enthusiasm for track and field. Shola practiced after school every day and on weekends, which meant that Nnenna's live-in playmate was not around much. Sparked by her sister's enthusiasm for running, Nnenna decided to join her at the Millrose Athletic Association.

Sibling rivalry being what it is, Nnenna's parents and Shola would all have preferred her to select another sport. However, as Nnenna reports, "My sister soon got over her grudge; in fact, running eventually drew us even closer together."

Nnenna's successes in track can be credited to the support of many people, including her coach, Barry Geisler; her sister, Shola; and especially her mother, "who, through nurturing, gave me self-confidence, self-respect, and the desire to use my natural talents."

I n addition to teaching Nnenna about her own stamina and talents, athletics have taught her something important about life. "As a runner, you constantly doubt yourself and your abilities," she says. "No matter how well you've done, you wonder if you can do it again or do it better. So I've had to learn to believe in myself and have the self-confidence necessary to excel. As a result, I'm constantly learning about myself and dealing with the issues of doubt and belief in myself in new ways."

LESSONS LEARNED

Self-assurance and confidence were essential when Nnenna began attending Villanova, a "powerhouse" school for cross-country. Overnight, she went from being the star of her high school team to one of many stars on the same team, which included former Olympian Vicki Huber.

"I tried not to think about being the best," Nnenna

remembers. "That is the kind of thing that puts pressure on people. The team title was all that mattered to me."

Actually, Nnenna's unwillingness to compare her performance with anyone else's took root early in her life. Her sister had already begun to make a name for herself in track, so for a while Nnenna was just "Shola's sister."

"At times, it was discouraging, and there were a couple of times I lost my interest in track and quit," she says. "Hanging out with friends became more important. But I came to a point—freshman year in high school—when I spontaneously dedicated myself to track, and I have not regretted it since. It earned me full scholarship offers to a myriad of colleges, including Villanova."

Nnenna's commitment to being her best has helped her to learn about the importance and rewards of commitment, dreams, and self-confidence. It also has enabled her to endure the pain, discomfort, and adverse conditions that accompany athletics.

"One of my assets is having a relaxed, one-step-at-a-time attitude," Nnenna says, "I don't mean that anyone should expect it to be fun at every step of the way—training is often not very fun at all! But I think it's important to have a sense of yourself, and to feel like a complete person independent of what you do—in my case, running."

What advice would she give to others who might take their talents too seriously? Nnenna believes that balance is the key. "Don't place too much significance on your sport, hobby, project—whatever the endeavor," she suggests. "Don't let it rule your life. It can lead to unhealthy behavior when your whole life is focused on one thing.

"Also, never identify yourself by what you do or by your accomplishments. This is very easy to do, especially when you've met with success. I am not 'Nnenna the runner,' I am 'Nnenna who runs.'"

As self-assured as she is about her athletic achievements, Nnenna has yet to choose her college major. Some possibilities include economics, political science, and sociology. Her only "definite" is a minor in business.

But whatever career she decides on—she has also considered becoming a teacher—there is one aspect that is not negotiable. "The 9-to-5 thing is not for me," she insists. "I will avoid it at all costs."

Having grown up in New York City, Nnenna seems acutely aware of the environment around her, and what she sees is not always pretty. "My generation has been handed down a slew of problems—the economy, drugs, AIDS, the eroding environment, and the overwhelming numbers of impoverished and homeless people in this nation—more specifically, the fact that the majority of Black Americans live in poverty. My ideals and sense of responsibility make me want to correct these problems."

Her wish for her student colleagues at Villanova? "That they'd become more aware of their world. They are pathetically apathetic to all issues except their social lives."

Finally, Nnenna wishes that everyone would realize that we are all "brothers and sisters. And I wish that greed and the insane things it leads people to do could be eliminated."

Harmony and peace: ingredients for global improvement.

Questions to Consider

1. Like many people who eventually succeed, Nnenna had moments of self-doubt, both about her talents and her desire to use them. In what area(s) do you excel, and have you ever felt this same sense of self-doubt? What specific things have you done to address your self-doubt? If you decided to pursue a particular talent, are you pleased with your decision? Why or why not? If you decided *not* to pursue your talent, how do you feel about your decision?

2. (This question is for people who have siblings—brothers and/or sisters.) Nnenna and Shola were in direct competition with each other. Have you ever been in direct competition with one of your siblings? Describe the situation. Discuss how you feel, how your brother or sister feels, and how your parents feel about the benefits and drawbacks of sibling competition and comparison.

Resources

You can read more about Nnenna in *The New York Times*, June 24, 1989, edition. See the article by Al Harvin on page 43, column 4, called "Pioneer, Champion, Honoree: Senior at Hunter High Follows Her Sister's Speedy Example."

Visit your library, and you'll find dozens, even hundreds of books about sports. Look in the card catalog or microfiche to find a list of books that interest you (maybe about your favorite sport).

Or, if you don't know where to start, see if your library has the Be the Best Series (Troll, 1990). This series includes books about gymnastics, football, basketball, BMX bike racing, tennis, volleyball, swimming, and more. Each gives a history of the sport, explains exercises and drills you can do, tells you how to get ready to play, and so on.

The Random House Book of Sport Stories, edited by L.M. Schulman (Random House, 1990), is a collection of fictional stories about all kinds of sports, from running to martial arts, many written by well-known authors.

If you're good at sports, like Nnenna is, and if you plan to go to college someday, it's not too soon to start thinking about scholarships. If there are colleges you're already interested in, ask them what they offer. Or check the *Chronicle Sports Guide* (Chronicle Guidance Publishing, 1987), which lists the sports scholarships offered by most universities.

19

STANDING UP FOR ANIMAL RIGHTS:
The Story of Jennifer M. Engel

Fifteen-year-old Jennifer Engel lives in a second floor apartment with her twin sister and both of her parents. Except for a recent fire across the street, Jennifer says, "nothing much exciting happens in Mayfield Heights, Ohio," the town she now calls home.

The Engels have moved a lot before

now—the family has lived in Pennsylvania, New Jersey, Michigan, and California—but Jennifer has settled down well into Mayfield High School. She describes it as "a very good school academically," and says that "there aren't many things I dislike about it, except that there are no windows."

Jennifer is in the school's Honors Program, as is her sister. In fact, the two of them attend many of the same classes together. Like most siblings, Jennifer and her sister don't always agree. But, as Jennifer reports with her tongue in her cheek, "once we put aside our differences in religion, musical tastes, style of clothing, and choice of friends, we get along fine."

When it comes to her parents, Jennifer disagrees with them on everything from politics to her curfew. Still, the whole family has learned that fighting about these things won't change anyone's views. "So," Jennifer says, "our disagreements remain in the background, and we're a pretty normal family."

What about hobbies and interests? Jennifer has many, including about 20 pen pals worldwide, reading, playing the bassoon, listening to all types of music (from "hard-core punk to classical"), going to concerts, being with friends, and talking on the phone.

MAKING A DIFFERENCE

As you can probably tell, Jennifer has some strong convictions, and she's not afraid to let other people know what they are. One of her firmest beliefs is in the rights of animals. She does not eat meat and will not purchase or use animal products, like leather. And she actively protests the use of animals for scientific research.

So, in ninth grade, when Jennifer was told that she would have to dissect a frog for her biology class, she faced a serious dilemma. "Biology is the study of living things," she asserts. "That is what I wanted to do—to study a living creature, not one grotesquely laid out in a dissection tray."

Jennifer refused to do the dissection assignment. Instead, she came up with several alternative ways to learn the material, and presented them to her teacher, principal, and school counselor.

146   **kid**stories

She could use diagrams of a frog dissection, Jennifer explained. Or she could use computer simulations or plastic models. She was open to almost anything except dissecting a real frog.

After much discussion, the school personnel offered Jennifer what they saw as a compromise. She wouldn't have to dissect the frog, but she would have to take a test in which she pointed out the various organs in a frog someone else dissected.

"I found this unacceptable," Jennifer says, "because to me it was still saying that it's all right to kill animals. If I had taken this option, my earlier objections would not have been worth much."

Jennifer decided to present her ideas to the Mayfield School Board. But she did not go alone. For support, she brought along her parents, a former school superintendent knowledgeable about school politics, and a student from a nearby town who had been through this same situation—successfully—in his own school.

Also, Jennifer asked two members of the Network for Ohio Animal Action, Jane Holloway and Donna Robb, to attend the school board meeting with her. Not only did they agree to attend, but they offered to donate money to the school to purchase a computer simulation of a frog dissection.

With the well-organized help of so many supporters, Jennifer was able to complete her biology assignment in a way that didn't compromise her values. "The decision came from the superintendent," she says. "He said that I should be given a test from diagrams in *The Zoology Coloring Book*. And that is how it was handled. As simple as a word, it was cleared up."

Although Jennifer won her own case, she feels that her job is unfinished, as her school has not yet adopted permanent policy regarding dissection. She plan' work on that project in the coming school year In addition, through a school-based pro' called "Creating Our Futures," Jennifer has become head (Mayfield High School's recycling program. And since the Mayfield has no recycling program, she hopes that the efforts will be duplicated there.

When Jennifer reflects on her efforts, she realizes the important roles others have played in her success. Jennifer's mother, Pat, was able to get her daughter's presentation placed on the school board's agenda. And an organization called People for the Ethical Treatment of Animals provided Jennifer with strategies and materials for "making her case" to the school board.

Still, if she had it to do over again, Jennifer would do a couple of things differently. "I made the mistake," she says, "of waiting until I was in the course to object. I should have started far ahead of time to allow for debate and to leave the school officials less pressured."

Along the way, Jennifer encountered some people who were unwilling to listen to her views. When this happened, she went to the next highest level. "When I got to the highest, I tried my best to win them over, and I guess my best was enough," she recalls. By setting a precedent, Jennifer is aware that she has helped a lot of other students she doesn't even know. But she scoffs at those who call her "brave."

"All I did was stick up for what I believe, as all people should," she insists. "I didn't do anything special. I did something that should be expected of everyone."

Jennifer hopes that other students will follow her example and challenge school activities that go against their convictions. She realizes that such actions may not always be popular with other students or teachers, but insists that this is something we all have to learn to accept.

"What I would really like to say is that if you're different than everyone else, that's cool," she explains. "Don't change. Even if you're lonely or depressed, you'll always find someone to help you out of it, even though it might take a while. So hey! Go ahead and be as weird as you want!"

The respect that Jennifer has for animals, and her willingness to act on her beliefs, is an approach to life she would like others to adopt. "If everyone wasn't worried about border violations, and language barriers, and killing each other off just because they call themselves something else, the world would be a better place," she says.

Questions to Consider

1. An important part of Jennifer's story is that she did not have to "fight the system" alone. Instead, she got help and support from a variety of sources and people. What do you think would have happened if she had not gotten this help and support? What if she had stood alone in refusing to do a school assignment? Would her story have had a different ending? Explain and discuss your answer.

2. The use of animals in medical and other scientific experiments continues to be a controversial issue. Research the various groups that have expressed opinions on this issue. Discover the pros and cons of each position. Then debate the topic in a classroom or school-wide forum. (You'll be surprised at how strong the beliefs are on both sides of this controversy.)

Resources

Some 4 million U.S. high school students take biology courses each year. About 75-80 percent of them are required to participate in animal dissection. More than 3 million frogs are killed every year for dissection in high school biology classes alone. These are just a few of the facts on file at the Animal Legal Defense Fund.

In 1987, a student named Jenifer Graham refused to dissect a frog in her biology class—just like Jennifer Engel. Her mother, Pat Graham, worked with the Animal Legal Defense Fund to start a national, toll-free Dissection Hotline to help students caught in the "dissection dilemma." In its first year, the hotline got more than 15,000 calls from students, parents, and teachers. To learn more about the hotline, or to request a student handbook, write or call:

> **Animal Legal Defense Fund**
> **1363 Lincoln Avenue, Suite 7**
> **San Rafael, CA 94901**
> **(800) 922-FROG (that's 800-922-3764)**

The Student Action Corps for Animals is another organization that offers help and telephone counseling to students who refuse to perform dissection in school. This organization seeks to empower students to work for the animal rights movement. To find out more, write or call:

> **Student Action Corps for Animals**
> **P.O. Box 15588**
> **Washington, D.C. 20003-0588**
> **(202) 543-8983**

As Jennifer Engel and Jenifer Graham both learned, there are many alternatives to using real animals for dissections. Here are just a few:

The *Zoology Coloring Book* (Harper & Row, 1982) contains 107 detailed drawings of invertebrate and vertebrate animals. The illustrations are ideal for use in lab exams that require students to identify animal organs. (This is the book Jennifer Engel used to complete her biology assignment.)

Operation Frog is a computer simulation of a frog dissection, available for Apple II and Commodore 64 computers. It teaches about biology and anatomy without using a real frog. Check your local software store or write to:

Scholastic Software
2931 East McCarthy Street
P.O. Box 7502
Jefferson City, MO 65102

Biology Lab is another computer simulation, available for Apple and IBM computers. With this program, you can dissect a frog, earthworm, grasshopper, crayfish, starfish, clam, and perch. The program also includes tests. Check your local software store or write to:

Cambridge Development Laboratory
214 Third Avenue
Waltham, MA 02154
(800) 637-0047
(617) 890-4640

The Student Action Corps for Animals can give you even more alternatives to animal dissection. (Ask them about films and videotapes, for example.)

20

LESSONS LEARNED AT SUMMER SCHOOL:
The Story of Chad Gervich

"**I**'d never even had a crush on a girl until a few weeks ago. Her name was Scarlet Larson, and whenever I saw her coming down the hall my heart would pound, my palms would sweat, and I'd have the sudden urge to drop my algebra book, rush into her arms, and discuss the French Revolution.

Nobody knew about my crush on Scarlet except Kilroy, my Siamese cat. I tried to explain my feelings to him, but it's hard to discuss love with someone who's been neutered...."

So begins "The Life and Times of a Freshman Nerd," a short story about growing up in America. The author, 16-year-old Chad Gervich, lives in Iowa Falls, Iowa, a heartland town of about 6,000 people. He claims that he and his family are the only Jewish people in town, although E.T. (his family's real feline) "is a devout *Cat*-holic."

As you might guess, two of Chad's hobbies are writing and comedy. He won a statewide writing contest at age 10 with his futuristic short story, "Moya's Way." In this story, children are removed from their parents to be turned into little Einsteins by the government. Chad likes to write because "it can take you anywhere and let you do anything." He also enjoys acting, playing tennis, water-skiing, and hanging out with his friends.

MAKING A DiFFERENCE

Like most teenagers, Chad looks forward to that very special day that arrives each June: the last day of school! But during a recent summer, he was one of 80 students chosen from among 600 applicants to attend the three-week Iowa Governor's Summer Institute for the Talented and Gifted. Called IGI for short, this residential program brings bright high school students together to study math, science, the humanities, inventions, and more.

If he was so eager for school to end, then why did Chad apply to IGI? Looking back, even *he* isn't sure. His teachers and parents thought that he would learn a lot there, but Chad wasn't convinced that he wanted to spend his summer with a bunch of kids who "wore suits, taped glasses, and pocket protectors to school."

His friends wondered why he would apply to "Geek City," "Nerd Camp," or "Dweebville" (their words). Chad remembers, "They all said, 'It's summer. Why would you want to go back to school?' That question was one I couldn't answer easily. Even I didn't know."

What finally persuaded Chad to apply to IGI (and to attend, once he was accepted) was talking with his friend, Tawnya, an

IGI "veteran" from the previous summer. "She told me I'd have the best three weeks of my life," he says. "For some reason, hearing that from a friend was a lot more convincing than hearing it from parents."

At the end of IGI, Chad had to admit that Tawnya and everyone else who had encouraged him to go were right. "It *did* turn out to be the best three weeks of my life, and it wasn't even that much like school," he recalls. "It was more like a giant party with intermissions for little classes.

"IGI taught me to follow my heart, to do something because I want to, not because of what my friends say. It also taught me that anyone can do anything. It wasn't one single incident that taught me this, it was the whole three weeks—the things I did, the friends I made, the hell we raised. And of all of the facts that were pounded into my brain, that's the one thing I know I'll never forget."

Chad's experience at IGI gave him an attitude towards life that continues today, and one that he feels should be shared by others who question their own beliefs, dreams, or goals. "You'll never get a medal if you don't run the race," he advises, "and you'll never get to the top of the tree if you don't go out on a limb. Don't worry about what other people might say—just do it!"

Something else Chad learned was that if you're going to take someone's advice, you'd better be sure the people who give it are worth listening to in the first place. Tawnya, for example, had gone to IGI herself, but none of Chad's other friends had, so how could they say it would be Geek City? Also, both Chad's teachers and parents had known him for several years, so he was willing to give their comments some consideration.

But Chad was 15, an age when all advice is viewed with some suspicion. This made him doubt the merit of his parents' comments. "I think a lot of parents have forgotten what it's like to be a kid," he says. "Most kids don't plan their free time around educational activities. Like lots of kids, I'm more worried about wearing clothes that make me look cool today than having an

kidstories

'educational experience' that will help me 30 years down the road. That may sound shallow, but it's the truth."

Chad thought it over. He finally decided that going to IGI would be in his own best interests. In fact, it was, from everyone's point of view.

PERSONAL
GOALS,
GLOBAL
CONCERNS

As he heads towards college, and a planned career as a stand-up comic and a writer, Chad is looking towards a future that will be enjoyable to himself and his audiences.

"A career should be as much fun as it is work, especially in today's go-go-go world," he explains. "Most people are in too much of a hurry going from here to there and back again to stop and smile. Maybe I can put back a few grins on a few faces."

Chad has this to say to citizens of the world who want to improve our planet: "Chill out and relax a little! There are people who have heart attacks at 35 because they can't take five minutes out of their day to have a Coke and a smile.

"If I could change the world, I'd make 'Don't Worry, Be Happy' the international anthem. There's more to this planet than office walls. Most people just don't know it."

Chad is enjoying his time as a teenager, and he has some advice for other people his age who seem anxious to become adults. "Don't grow up too fast," he tells them. "You only get one shot at being a kid, and you'll be grown up for 80 percent of your life. Why rush it? Adulthood may look great, but how many adults go out and cruise the loop on a Friday night? Or sneak into R-rated movies? Or have cheese ball fights in the middle of Hardees? You only get to be young once. Make the most of it. Have fun."

It doesn't take a genius to see that Chad Gervich is ready to take his own advice.

Questions to Consider

1. How would you describe Chad's philosophy of life? How does it compare to the philosophies of other students profiled in *Kidstories?* Do you think it really would be possible to maintain Chad's attitudes on a worldwide basis? Why or why not? How might the world be different if government leaders adopted Chad's casual approaches to life?

2. What's the real point of Chad's story? Overcoming the accusations of being a geek? Enjoying a summer school experience? Learning to listen selectively to people's advice? Developing an attitude toward life that allows kids to stay young as long as they want? What is the most meaningful part of Chad's story, when you apply it to your own life?

Resources

If you want to find out more about special summer camps, like the Iowa Governor's Summer Institute for the Talented and Gifted that Chad attended, contact your state gifted coordinator at your State Department of Education.

IGI wasn't all work; as Chad points out, he also had fun and made friends. IGI brought together many young people who had been identified as "talented and gifted." For Chad, it was an opportunity to spend time with other kids with abilities similar to his—kids who didn't think of him as a "geek," a "nerd," or a "dweeb."

Many talented and gifted kids feel as if they don't fit in with other students their age. They feel as if they're alone in the world—but they are not alone! If you want to know more about growing up gifted, Free Spirit Publishing has several books you may be interested in, including *The Gifted Kids Survival Guides* and *Gifted Kids Speak Out.* For a free catalog, write or call:

> **Free Spirit Publishing Inc.**
> **400 First Avenue North, Suite 616**
> **Minneapolis, MN 55401**
> **(800) 735-7323**

BIOGRAPHICAL SKETCHBOOK

Dear Student,

Have you accomplished something in your life that is important and exciting? Would you like to share your story with other students?

Kidstories is made up of stories about young people like you. If you will take the time to complete the "sketchbook" on pages 160-162 and send it to me, I might consider using your biography in a future book.

If your biography is selected, I will contact you again to get any extra details I need, as well as a photograph. And if your story is published in a future book, you will get a free copy.

As a teacher myself, I know how much I have learned from my students. The idea behind *Kidstories* is to show other people (for example, students, teachers, and parents) that they, too, can learn from students like you.

Thanks for your help. I hope to hear from you.

Sincerely,

Jim Delisle

Jim Delisle, Ph.D.
Associate Professor
401 White Hall
Kent State University
Kent, OH 44242

P.S. If the "sketchbook" is too long for you to complete by yourself, someone else can write down your ideas for you.

I. Some Basic Information

(Make a copy of this sheet, fill it out, and send it to me along with your completed "sketchbook.")

Name: _____

Age: _____ **Grade Level:** _____

Address: _____

_____

_____

Phone: _____

Did you find this form yourself at the back of *Kidstories*? Or did someone give it to you?

    ___ I found it myself

    ___ Someone gave it to me

    The name of the person who gave it to me:

_____

II. Description of Your School, Your Home, and Your Town

(Please write your responses on paper from this point on. It will help me if you identify your responses with the question number and letter—for example, "Question III, Part A.")

Please describe where you live and go to school, how many people are in your family (pets included!), and any interesting facts about your life (for example, that you've moved a lot, that you're the oldest of 15 kids, that you live with your grandmother, etc.).

kidstories

III. An Achievement That Makes You Feel Proud

A. Have you accomplished something worth sharing with other students? Please describe fully this project or activity or event, and explain how you got interested in this issue.

B. Who helped you in achieving this goal, and what specific things did they do to help?

C. What were the biggest problems or obstacles you encountered, and how did you overcome them? Were there any problems you could *not* solve, and what did you do about these?

D. How did you feel at the end of your experience, and what new things did you learn—about your topic and about yourself?

E. Is there any advice you could give to other students who would like to do something similar to what you've just described?

IV. Other Stuff

A. Please list and describe your hobbies and other interests.

B. What future plans do you have? Do you have any ideas about the careers you'd like to investigate? Why do these areas interest you?

C. If you could change something about 1) your school, 2) your neighborhood, and 3) your world, what would you change?

D. What else would you like to share with me or your readers?

Thank you for completing this "sketchbook." Please send it to me at 401 White Hall, Kent State University, Kent, OH 44242. Feel free to include newspaper articles, photographs, etc. if you wish (I'm unable to return items to you, so send copies).

One last thing: If you're under 18 years old, one of your parents/guardians needs to sign the bottom of this page so it's okay for me to include your story, if it's selected, in a book.

Thanks again!

_____
Parent/Guardian approval signature   Date

kidstories

INDEX

kidstories

kidstories

About the Author

JIM DELISLE

Generally, Jim Delisle is a professor of education at Kent State University. But during the 1991-1992 school year, he became an elementary school teacher in Solon, Ohio. Also, Jim is a writer and a counselor (sometimes). He enjoys the ocean, and his family. When he is at the ocean with his family, that is the most special time of all.